I0392625

Samantha Moore
Easy Mandalas

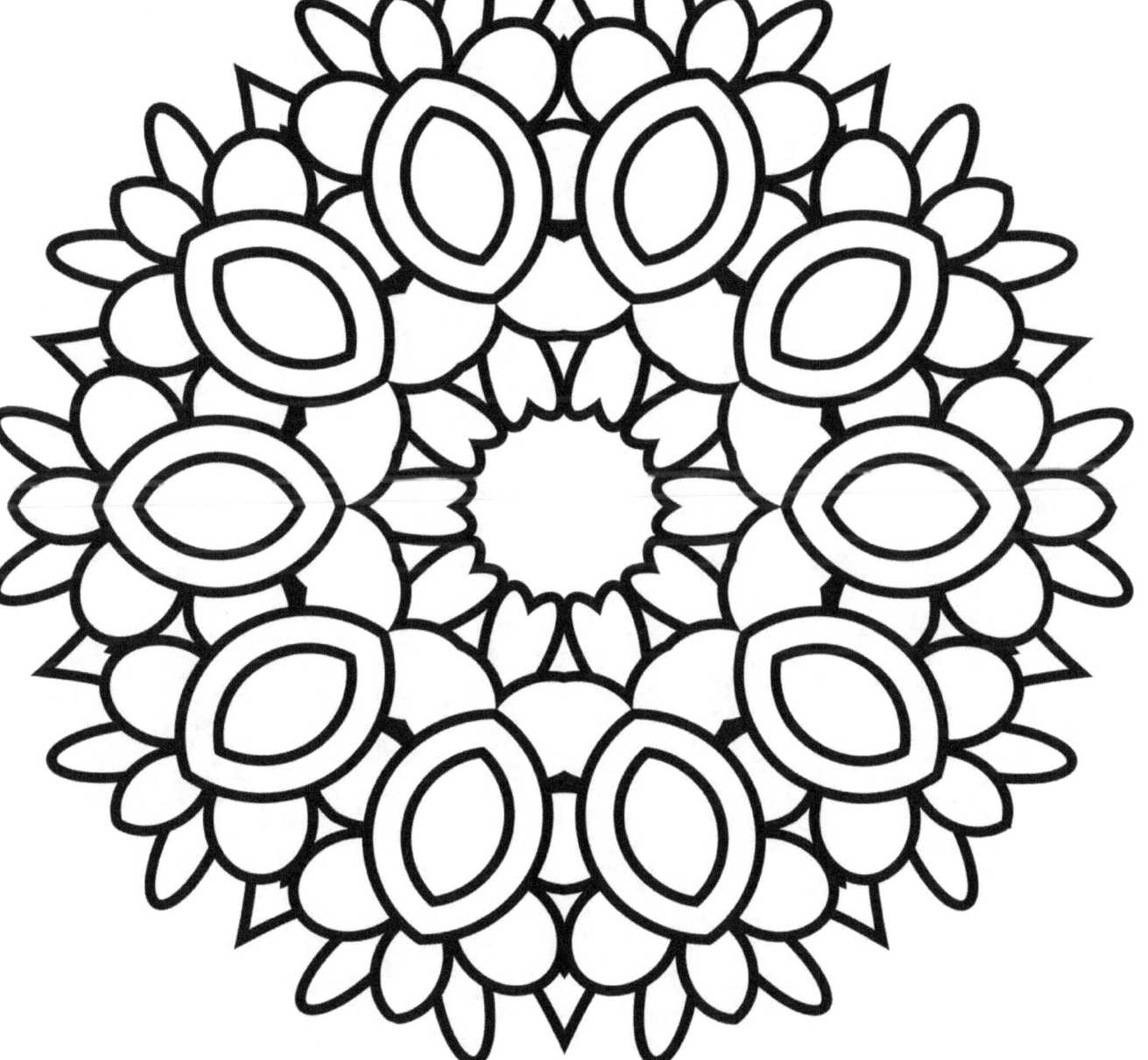

Adults Coloring Book
For beginners, seniors and individuals with low vision

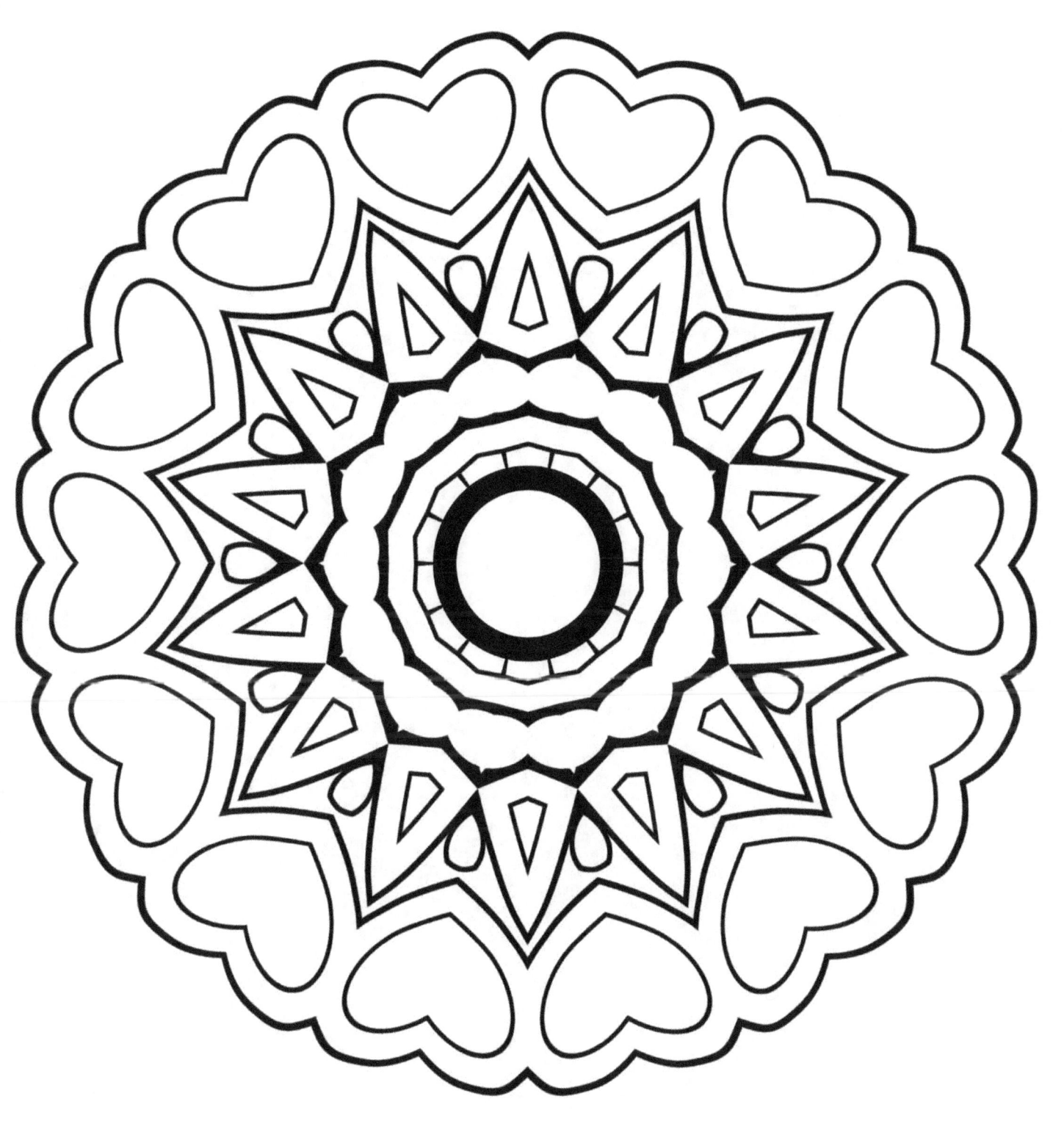

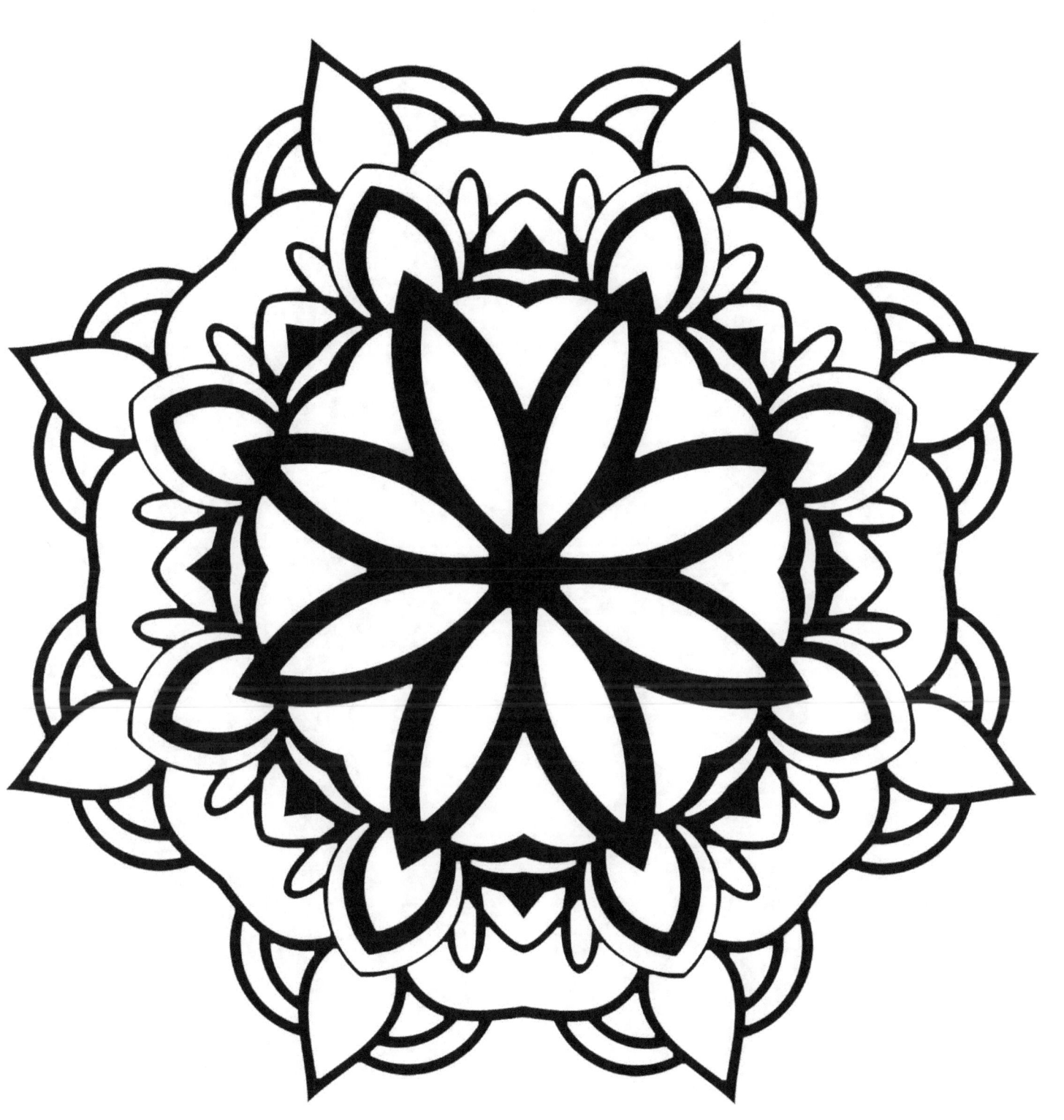

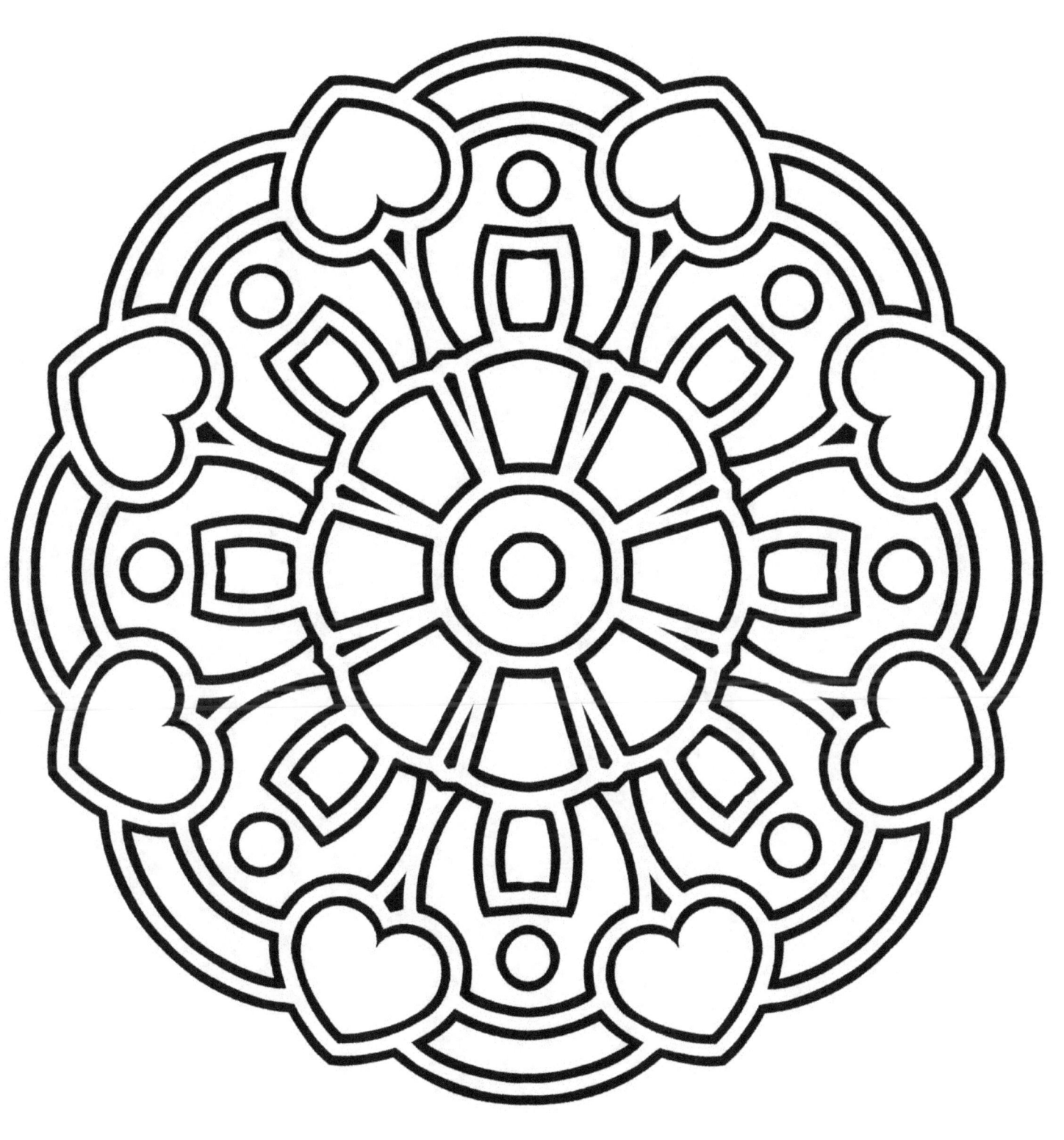

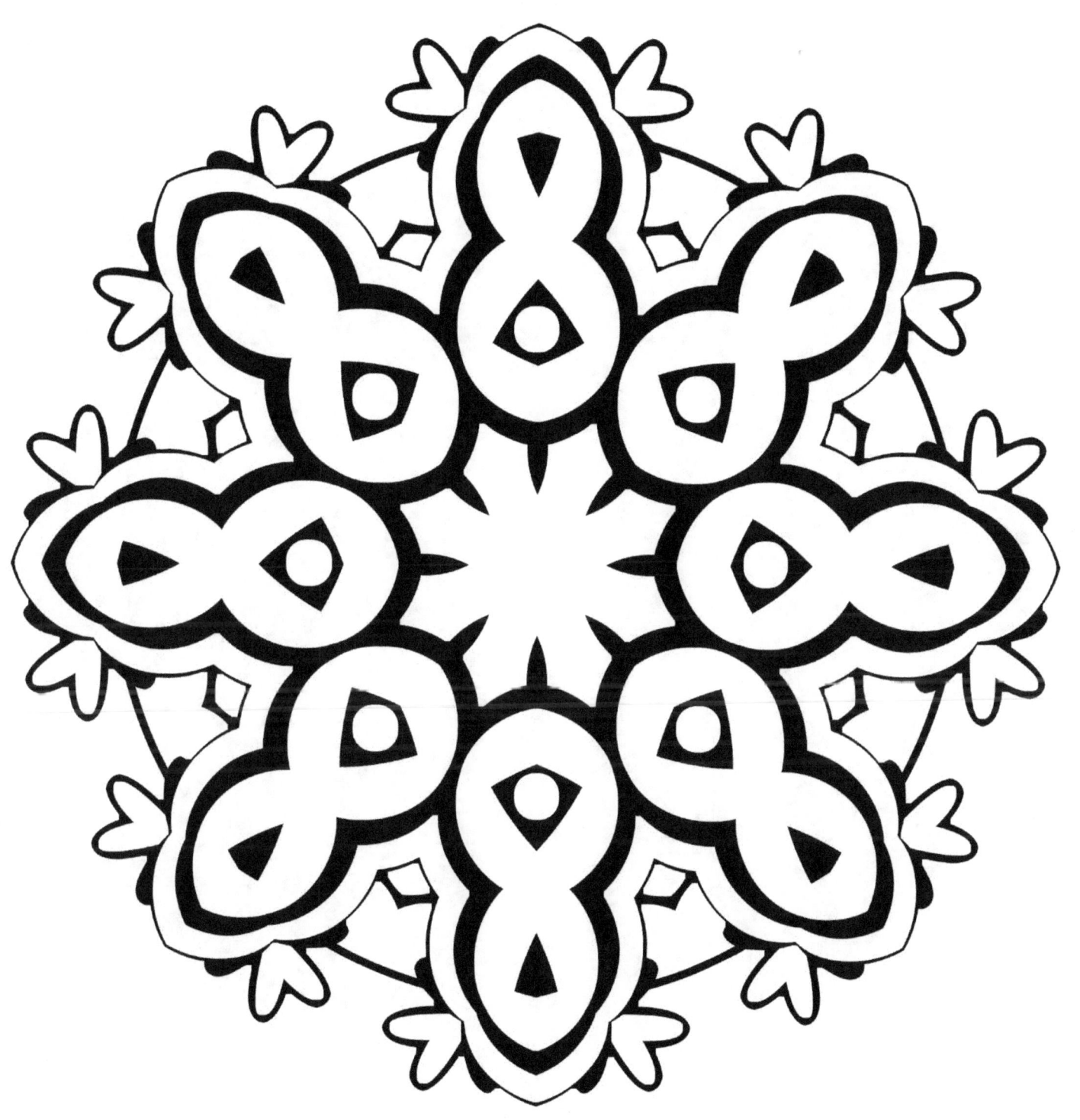

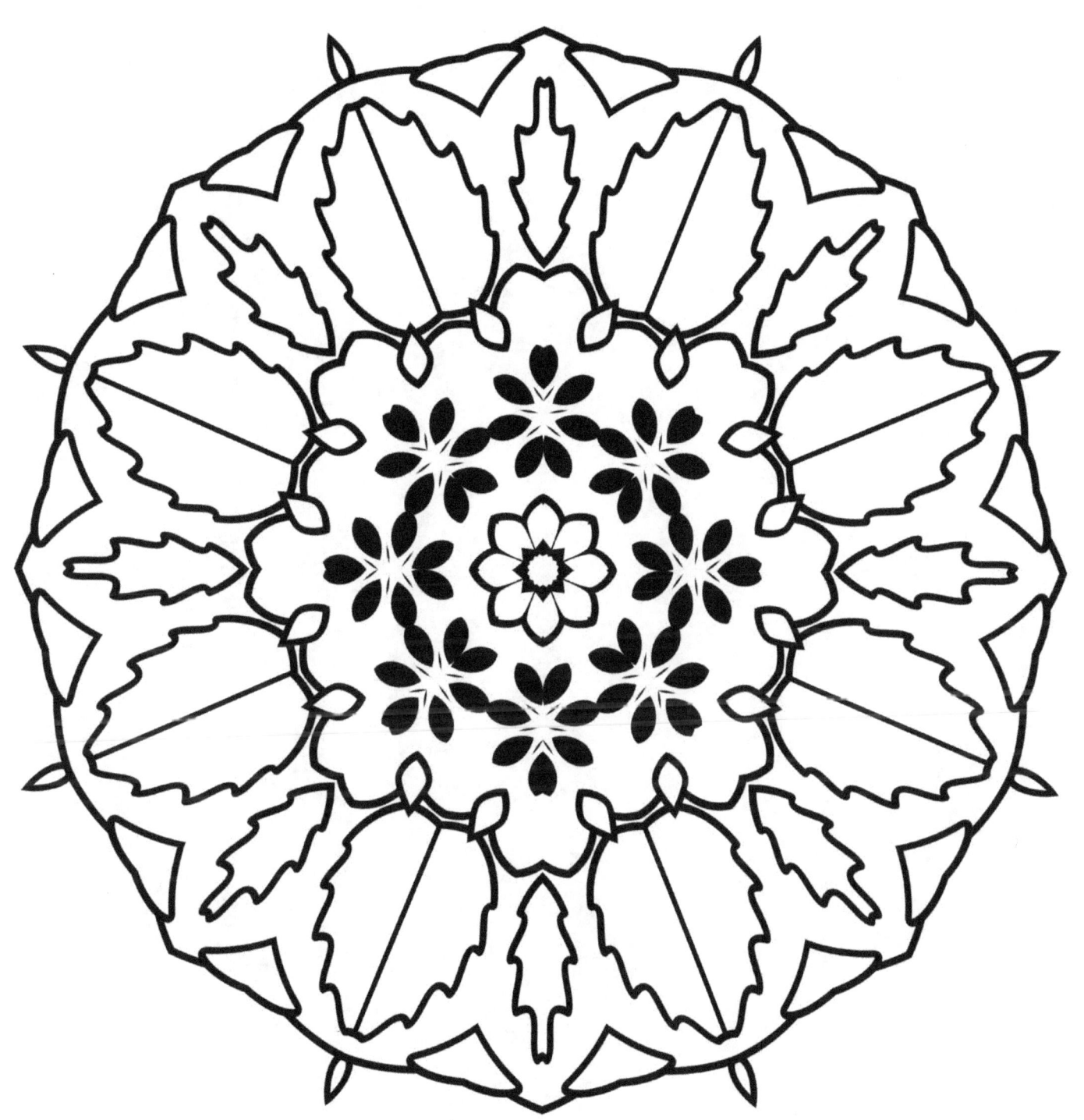

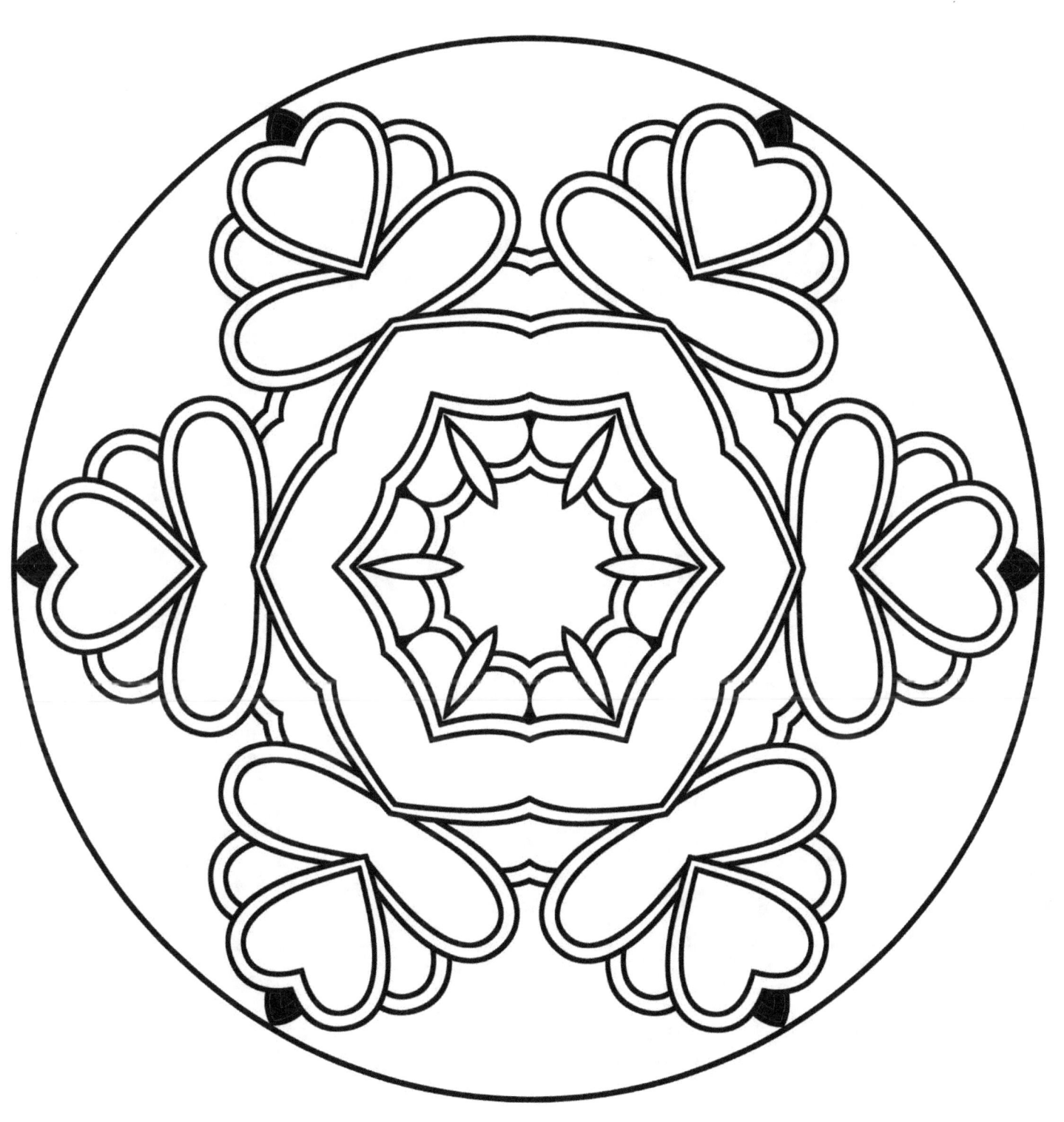

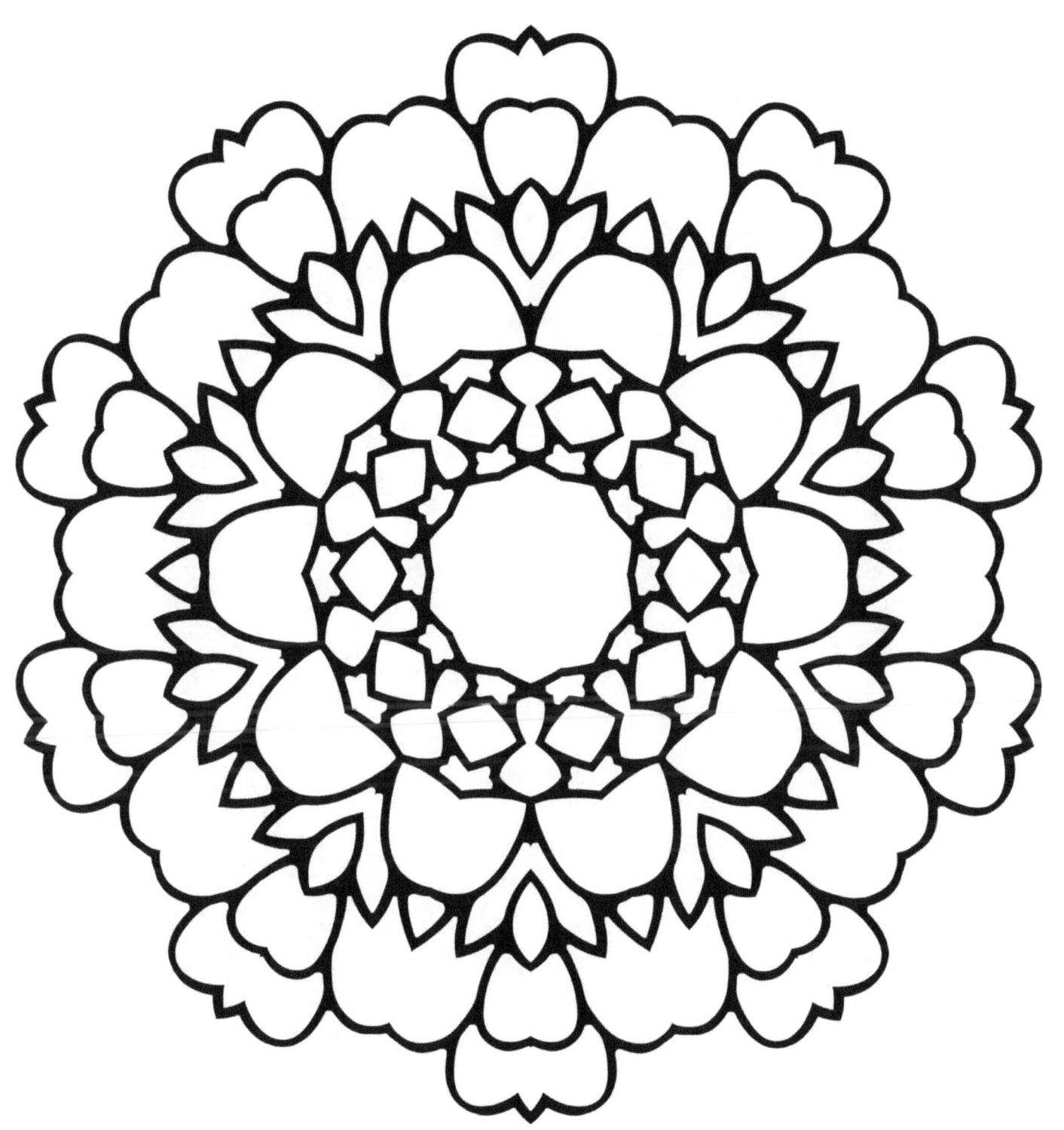

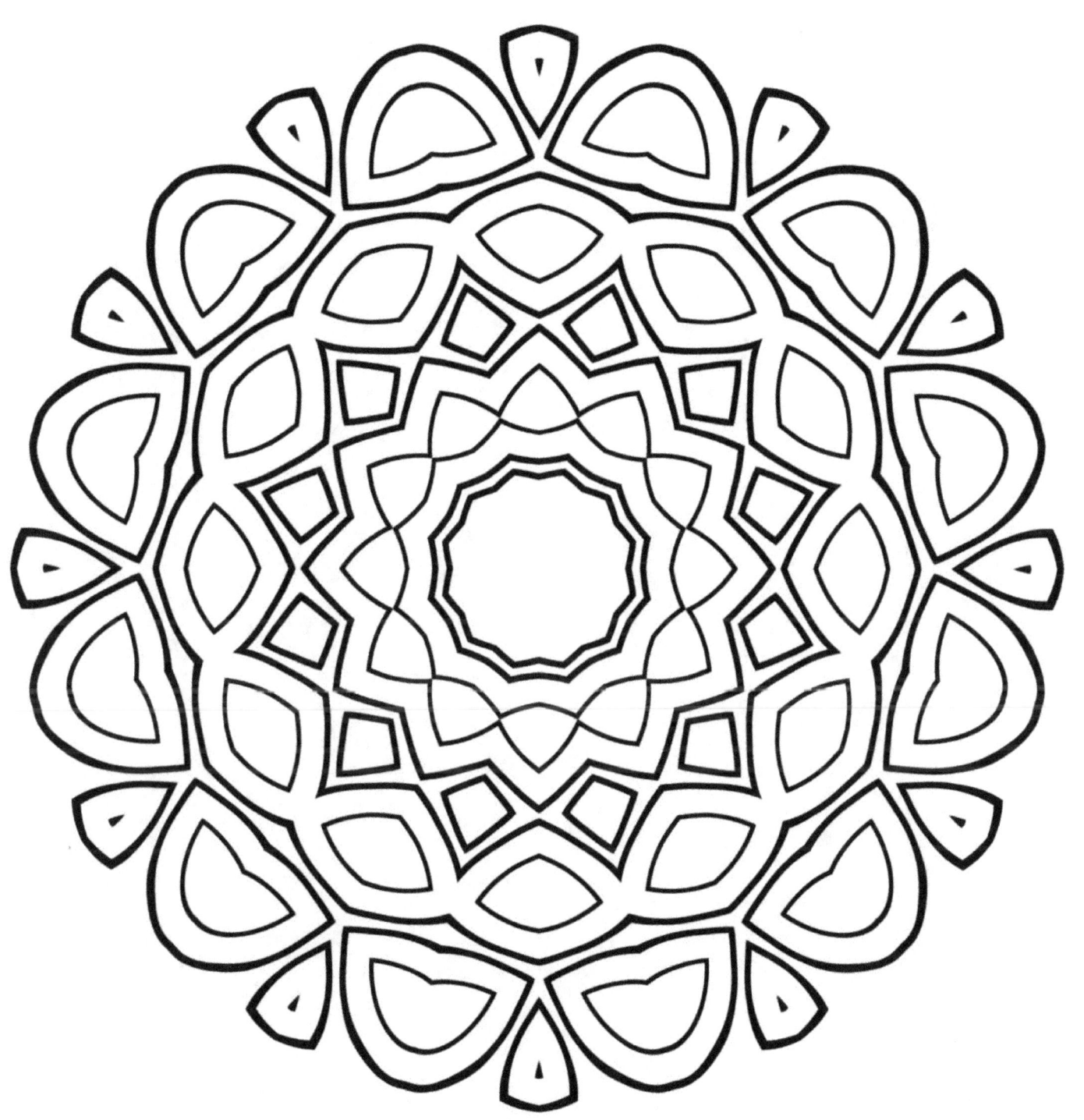

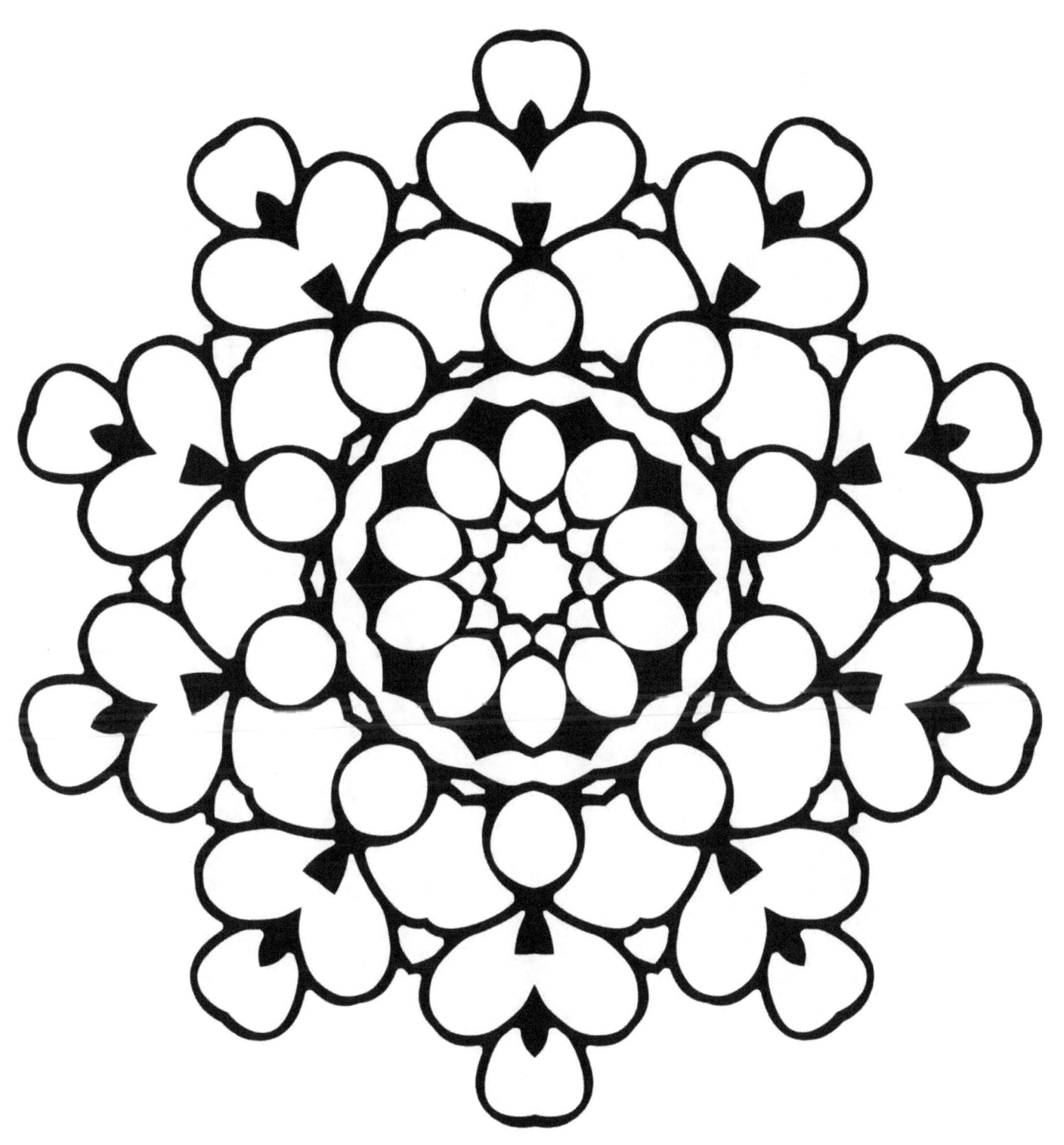

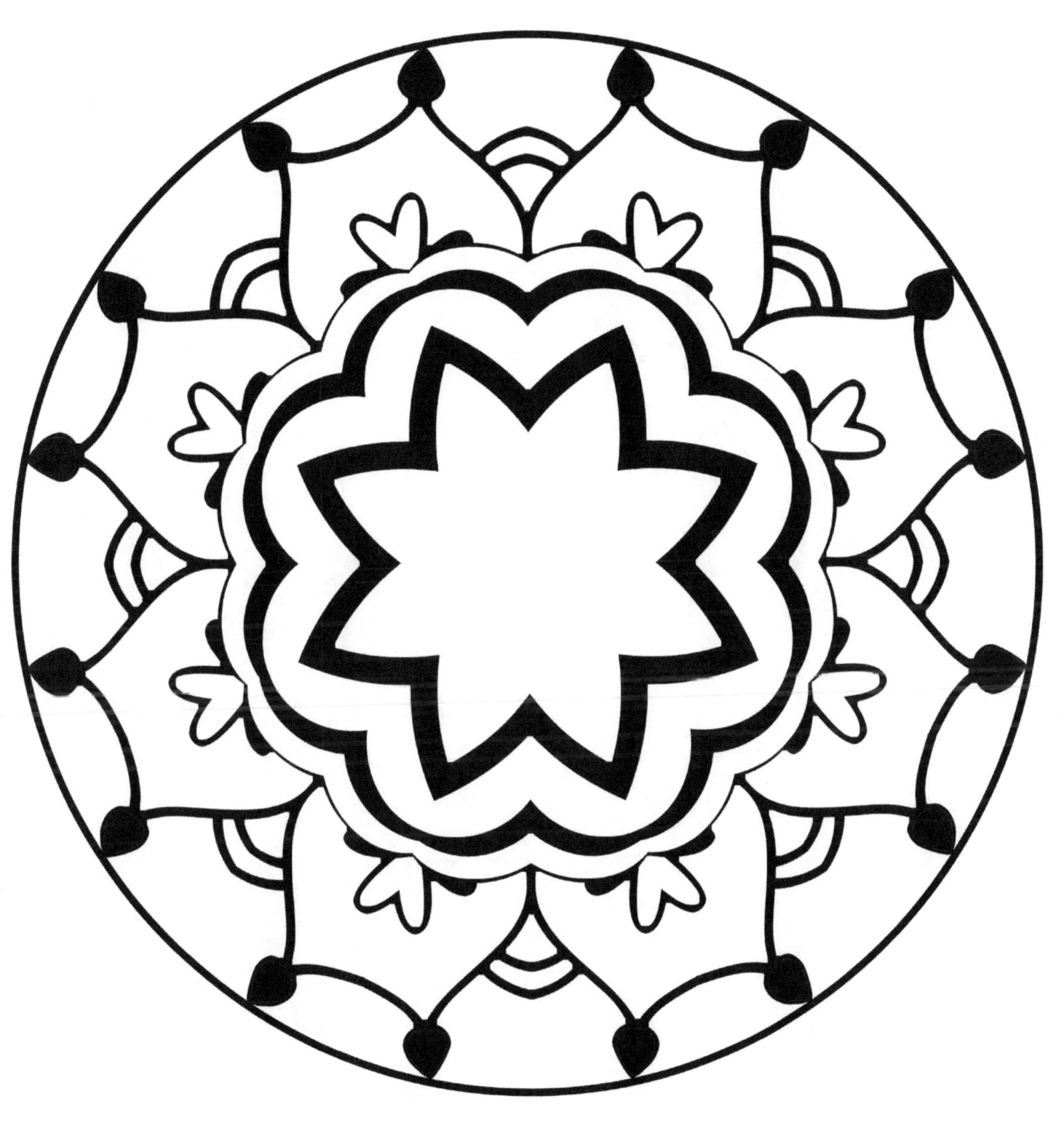

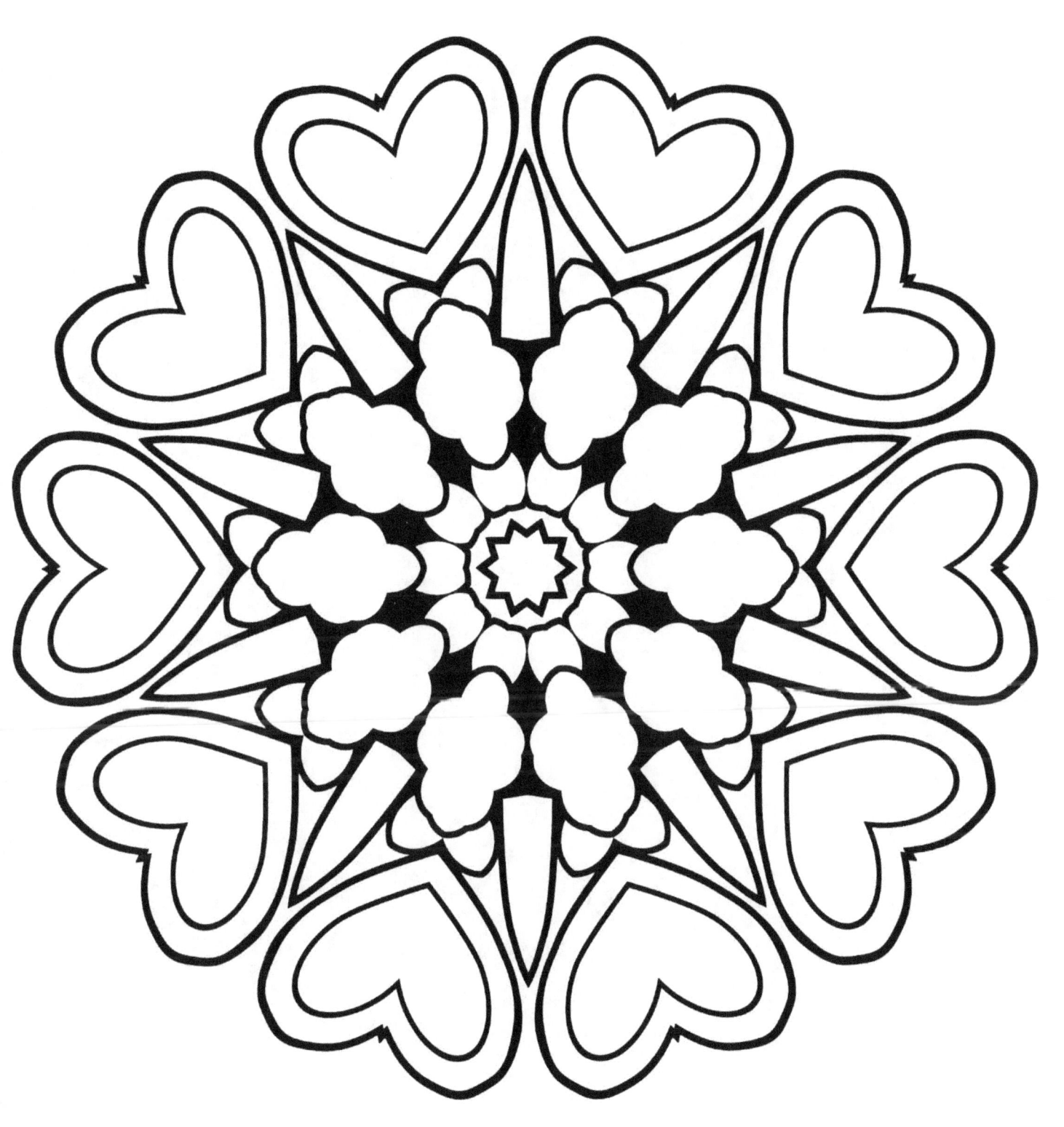

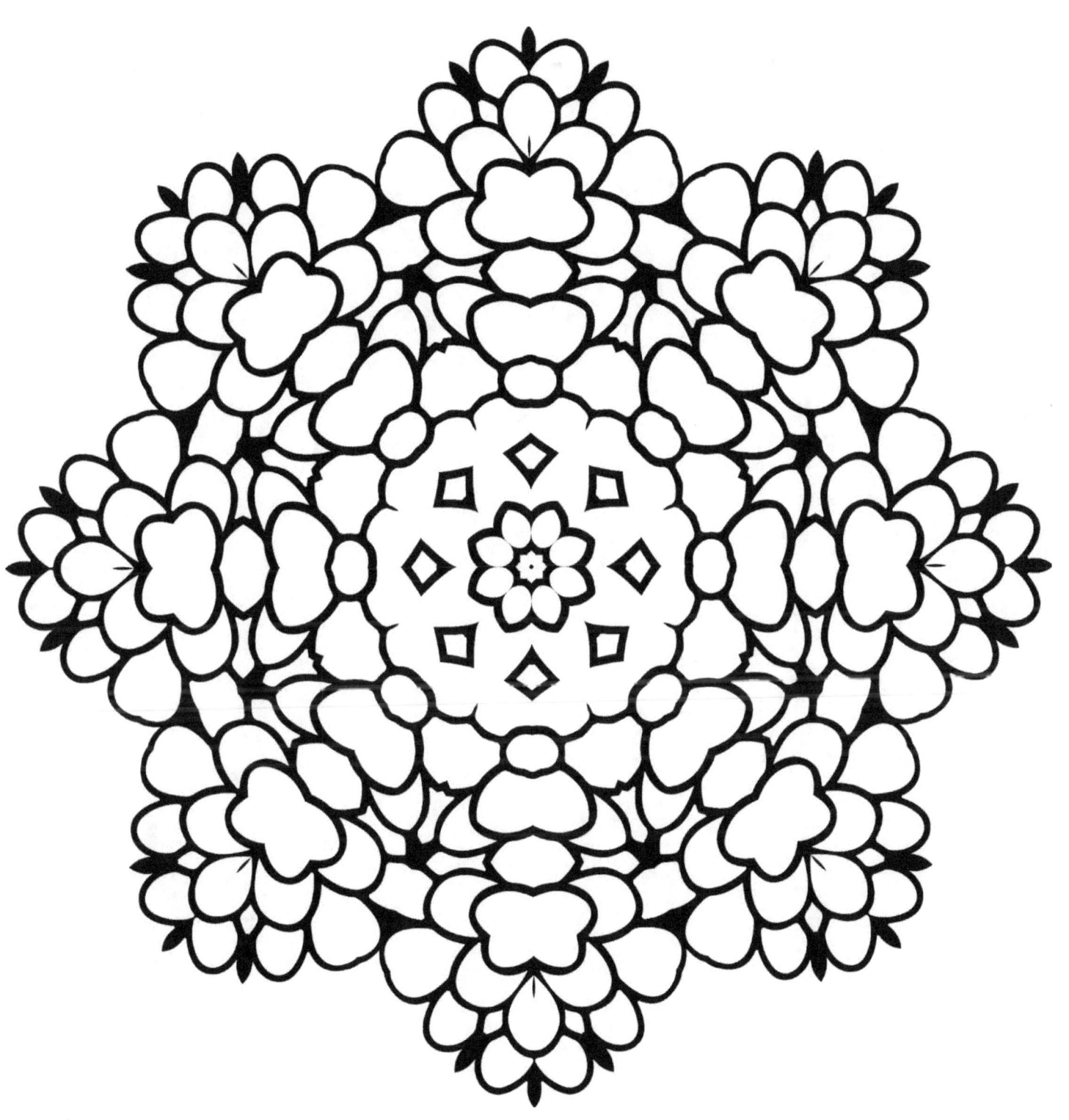

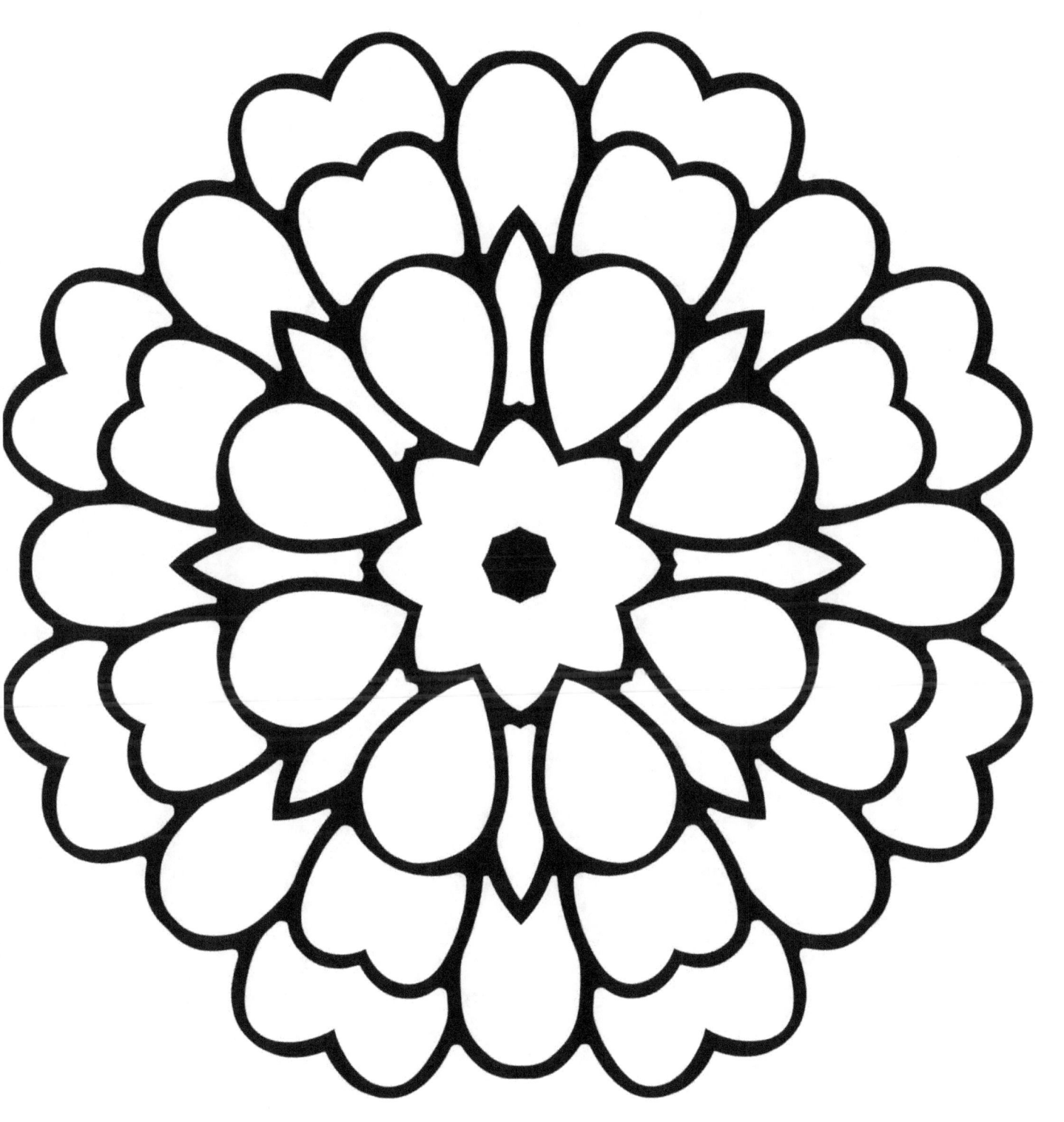

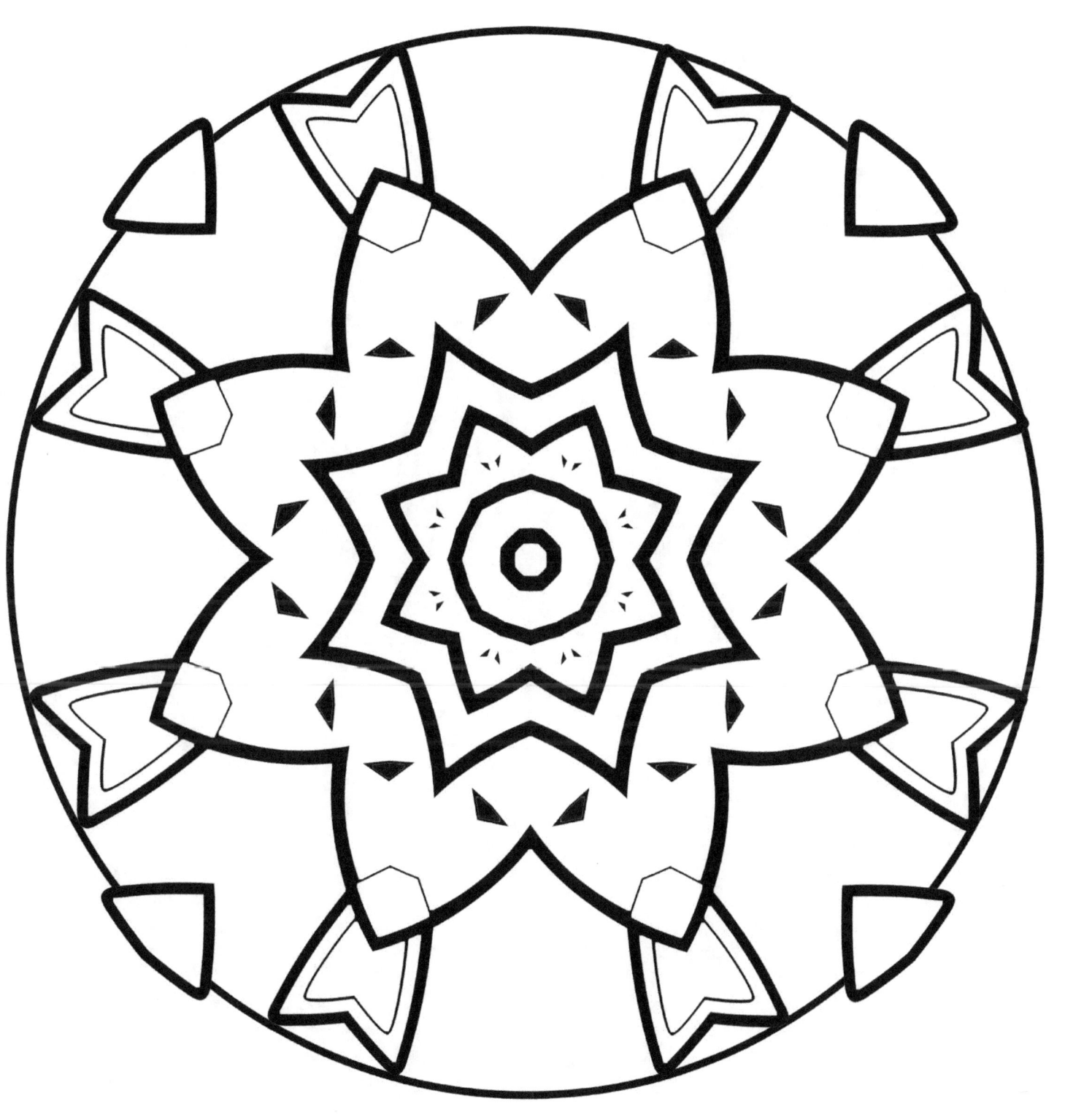

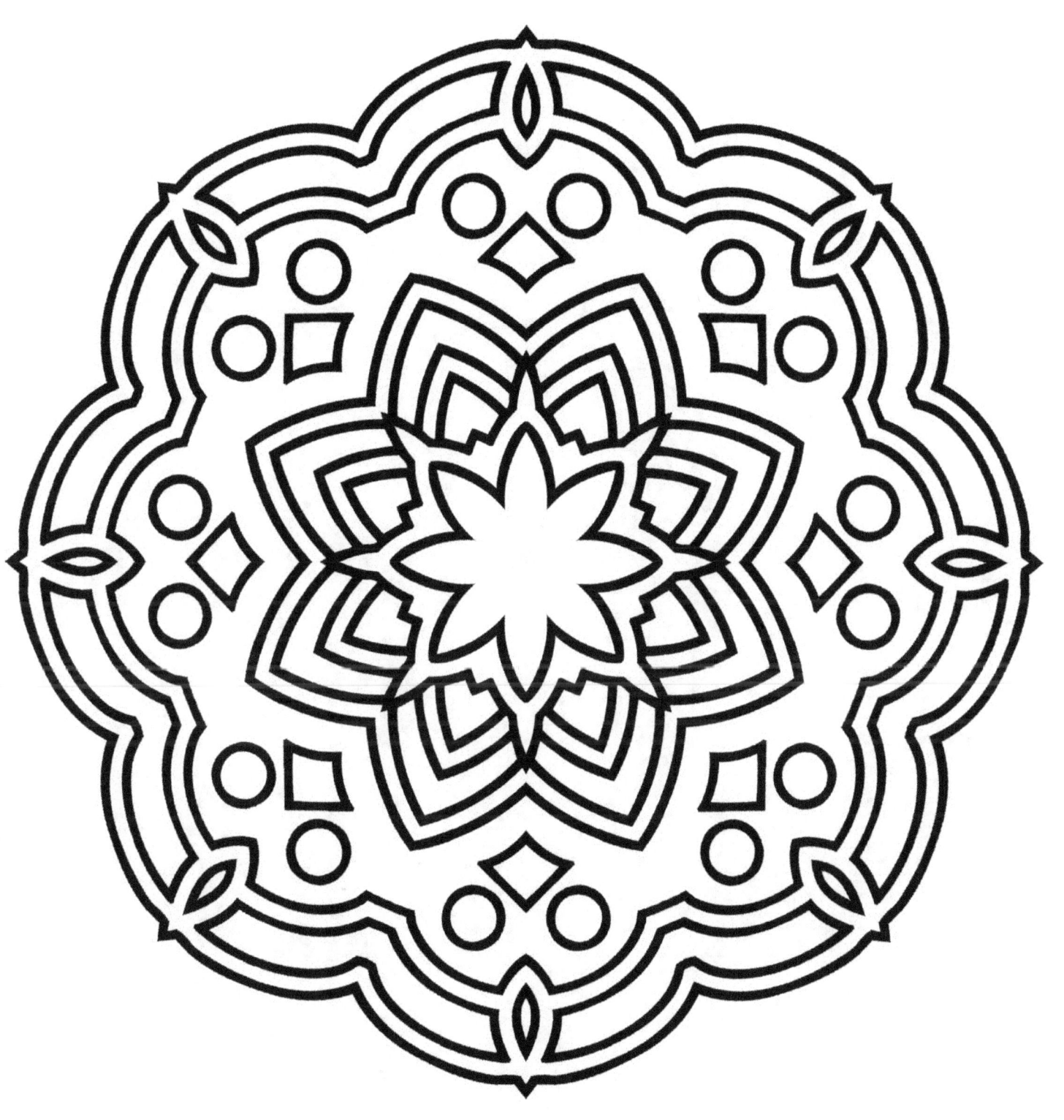

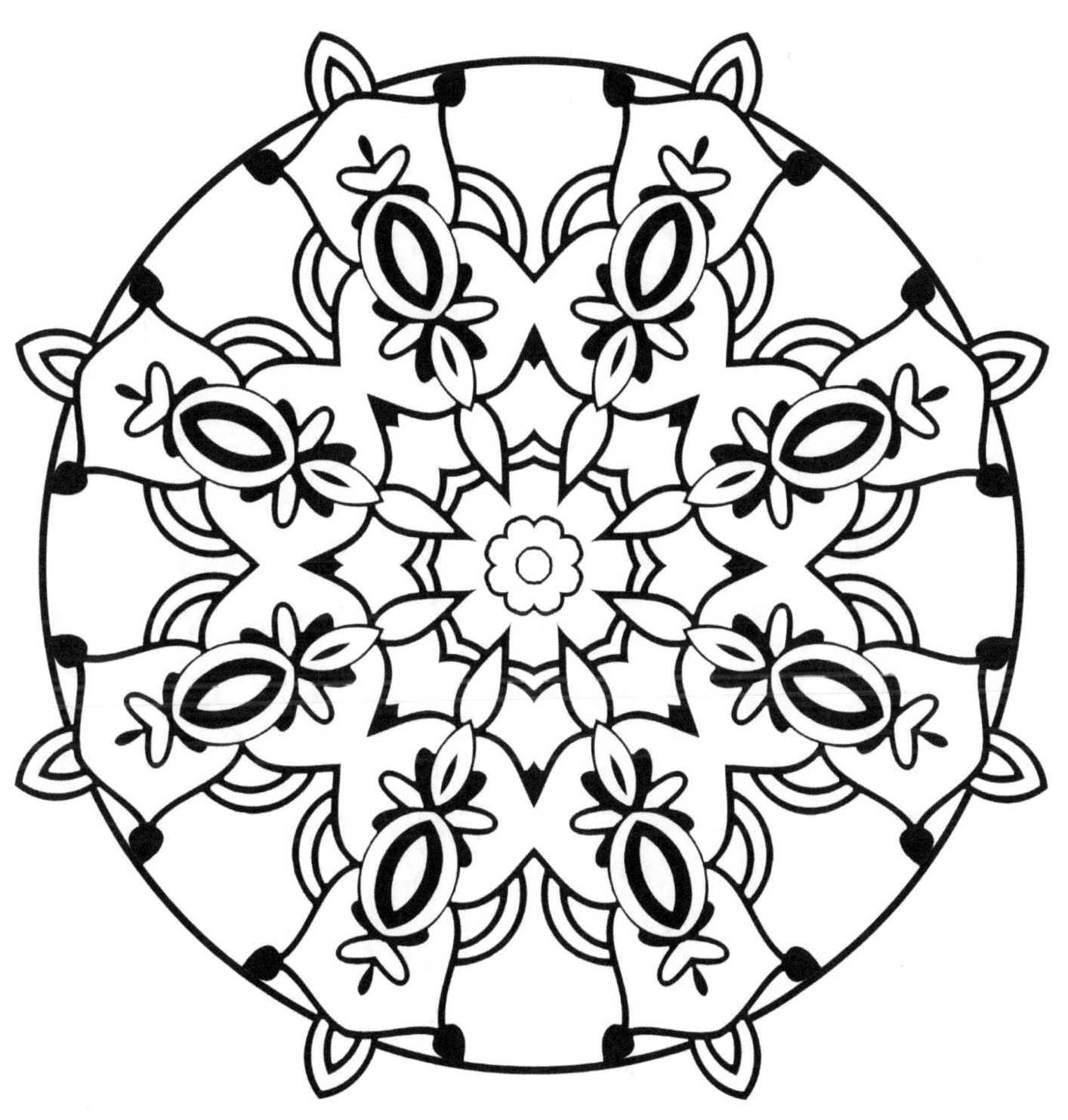

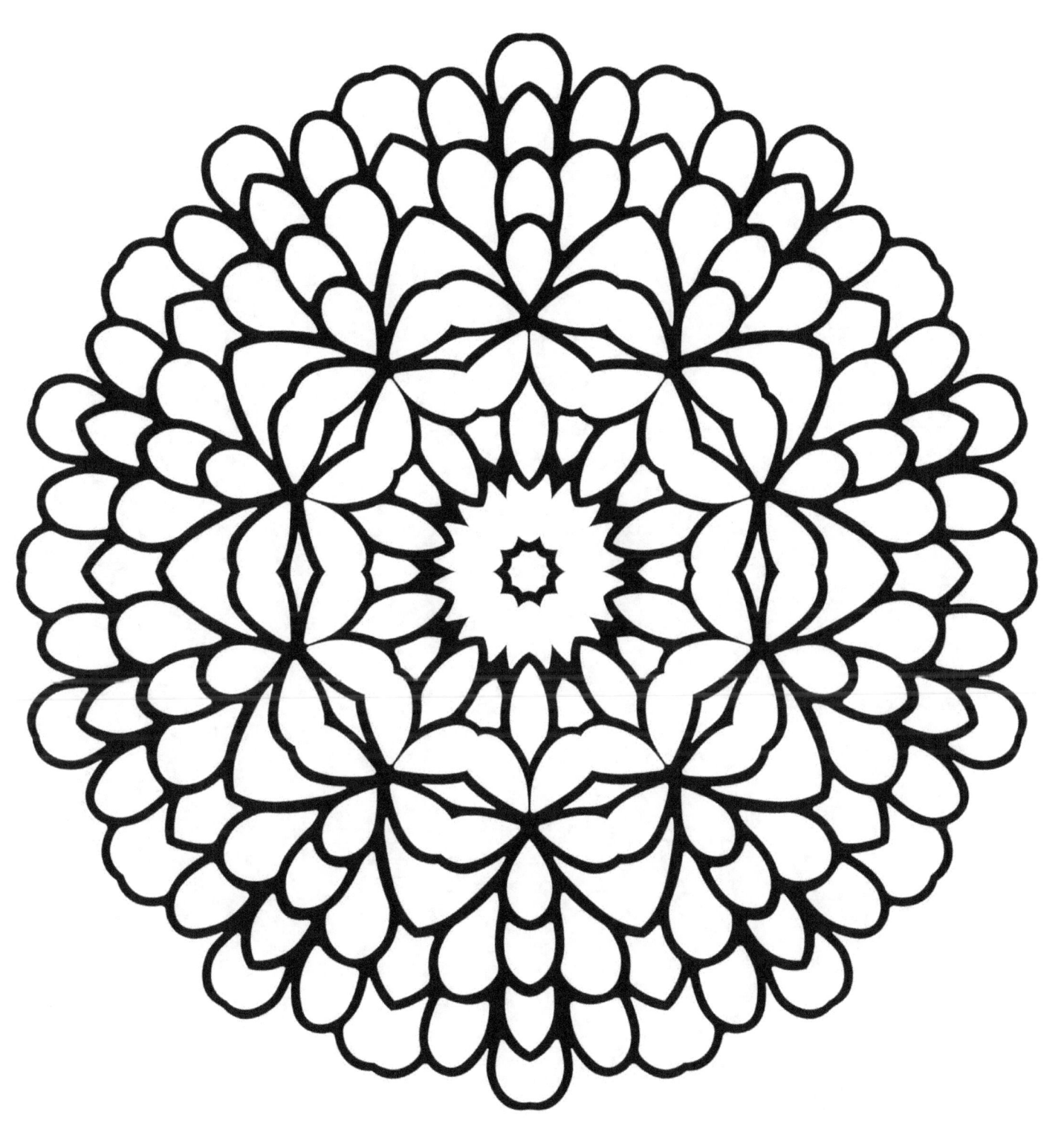

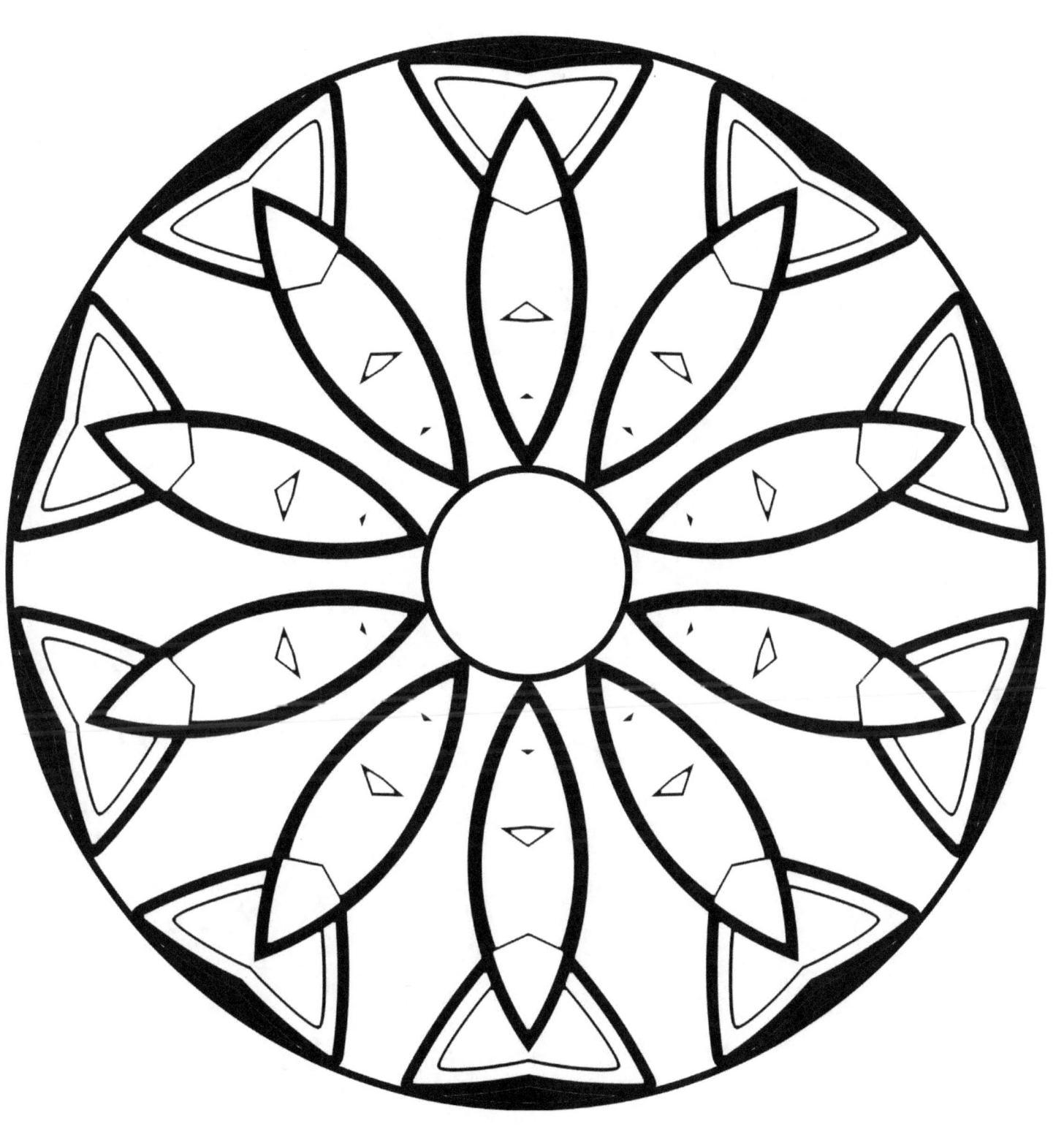

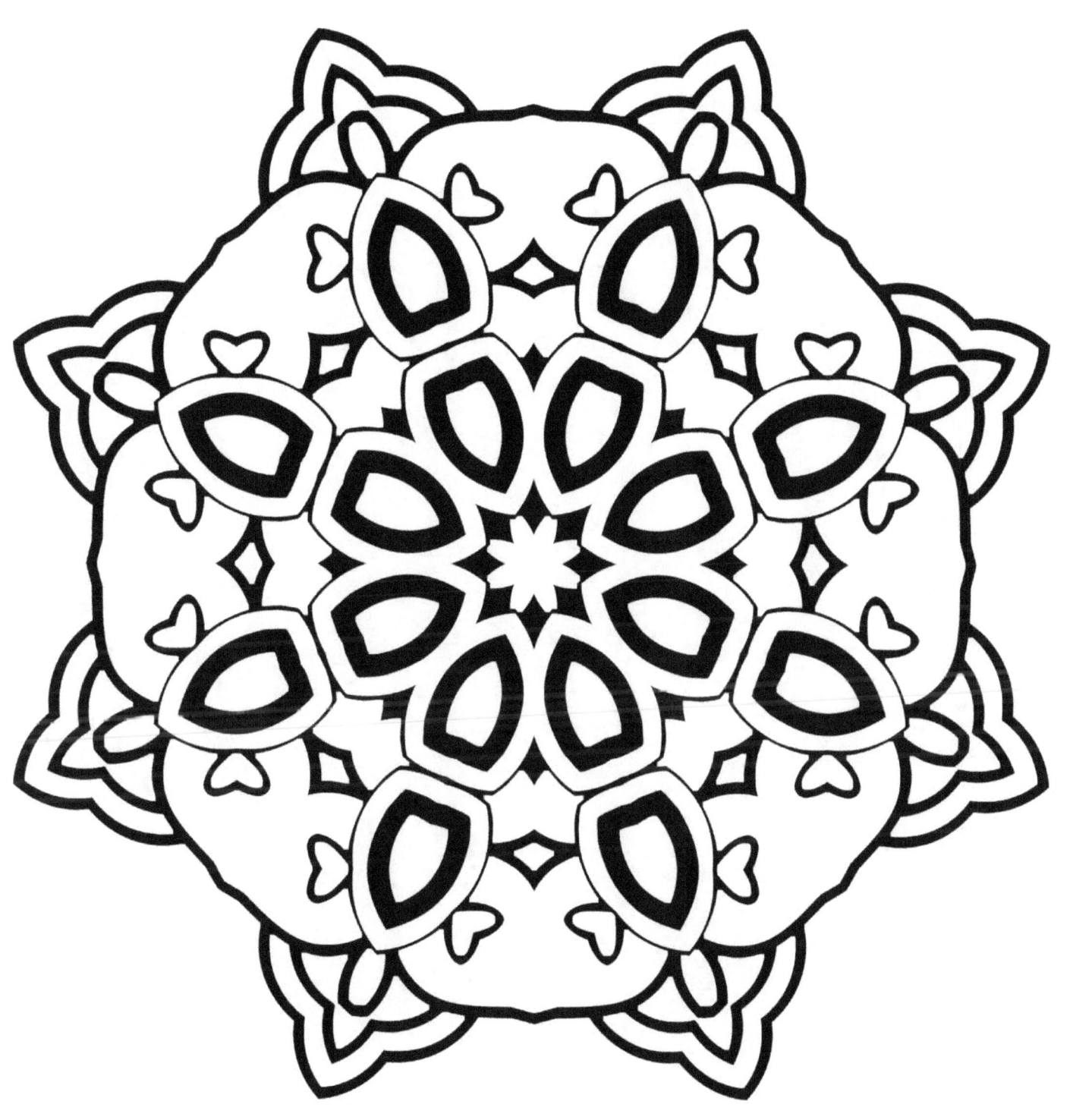

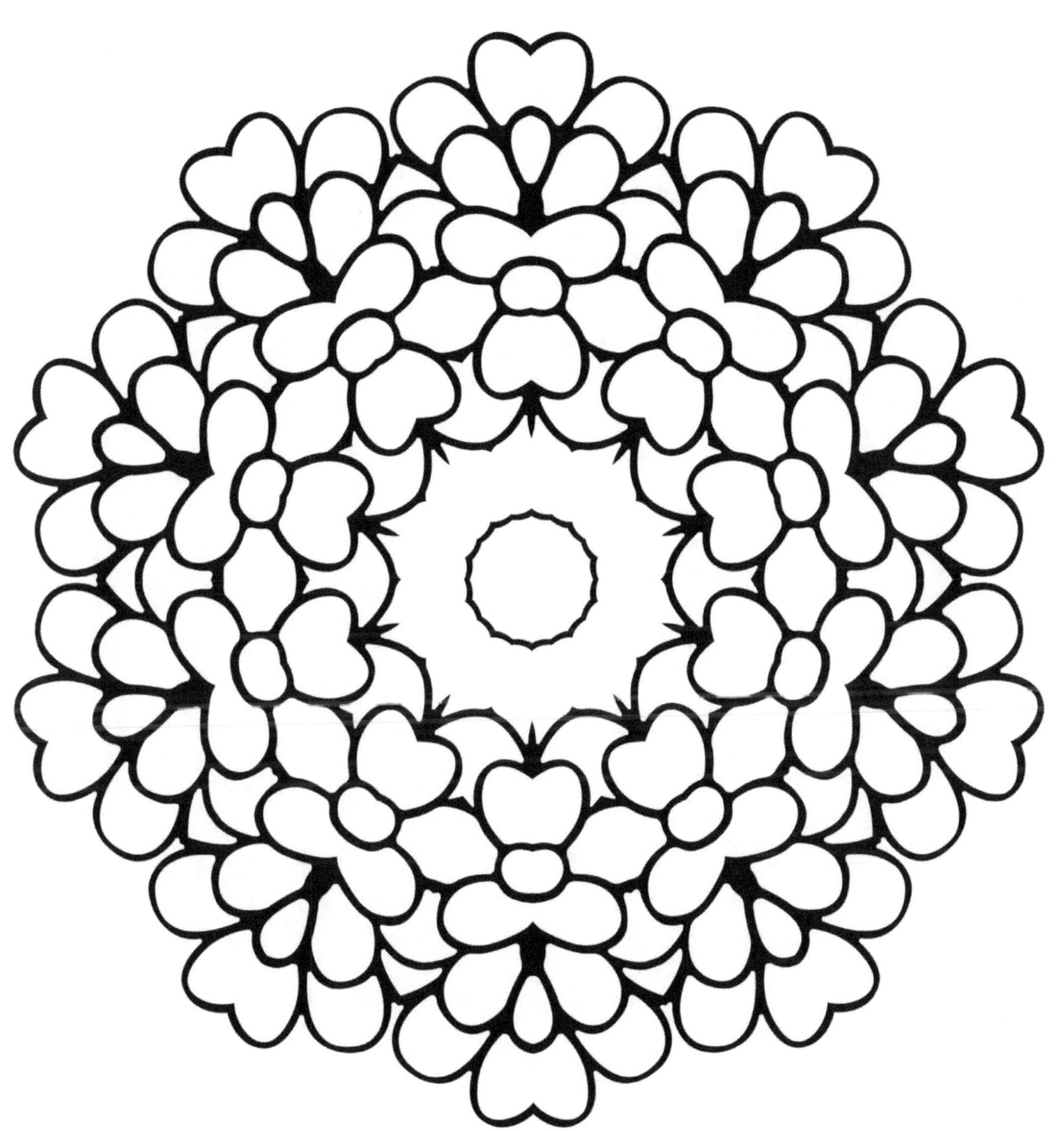

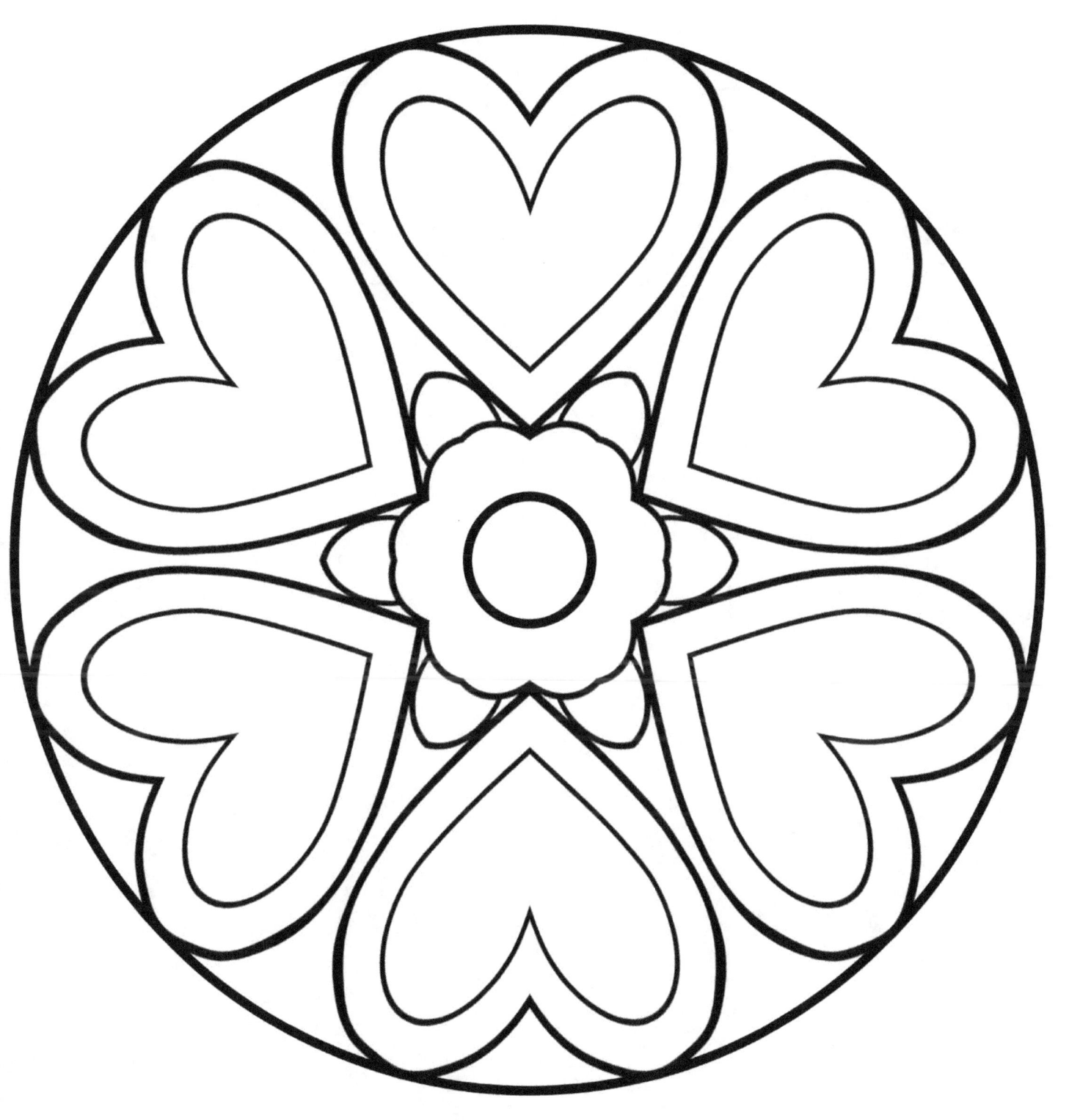

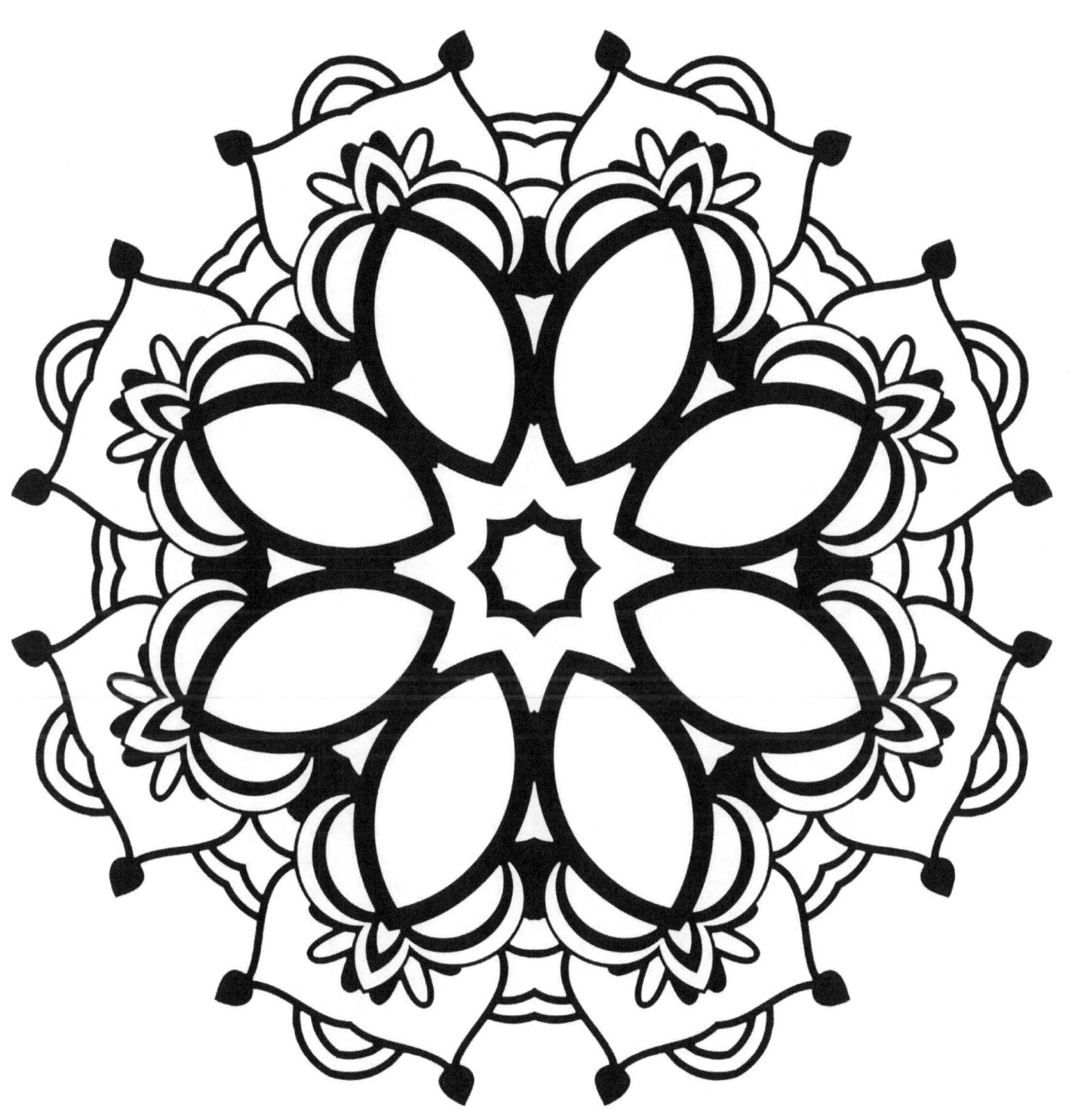

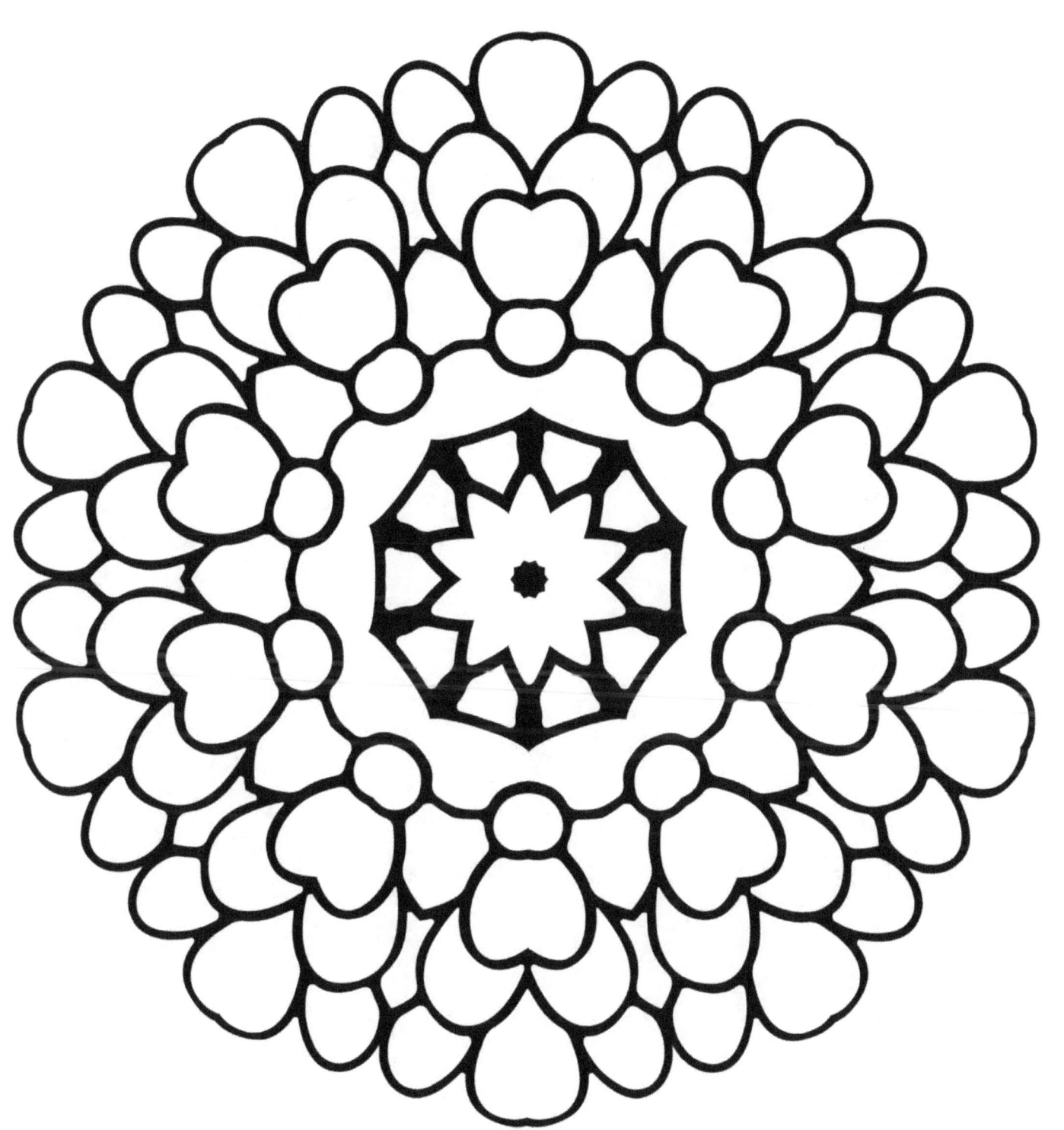

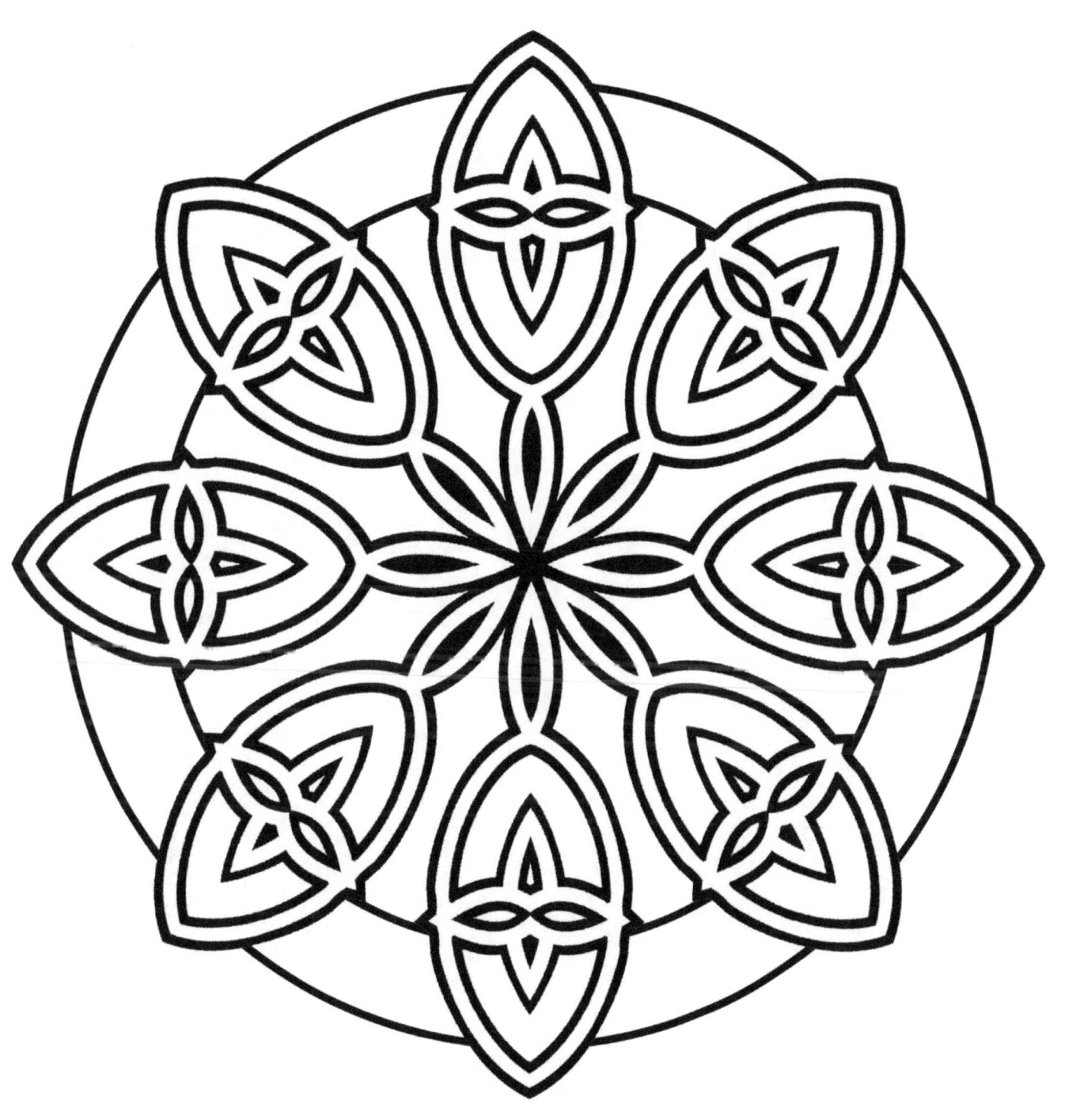

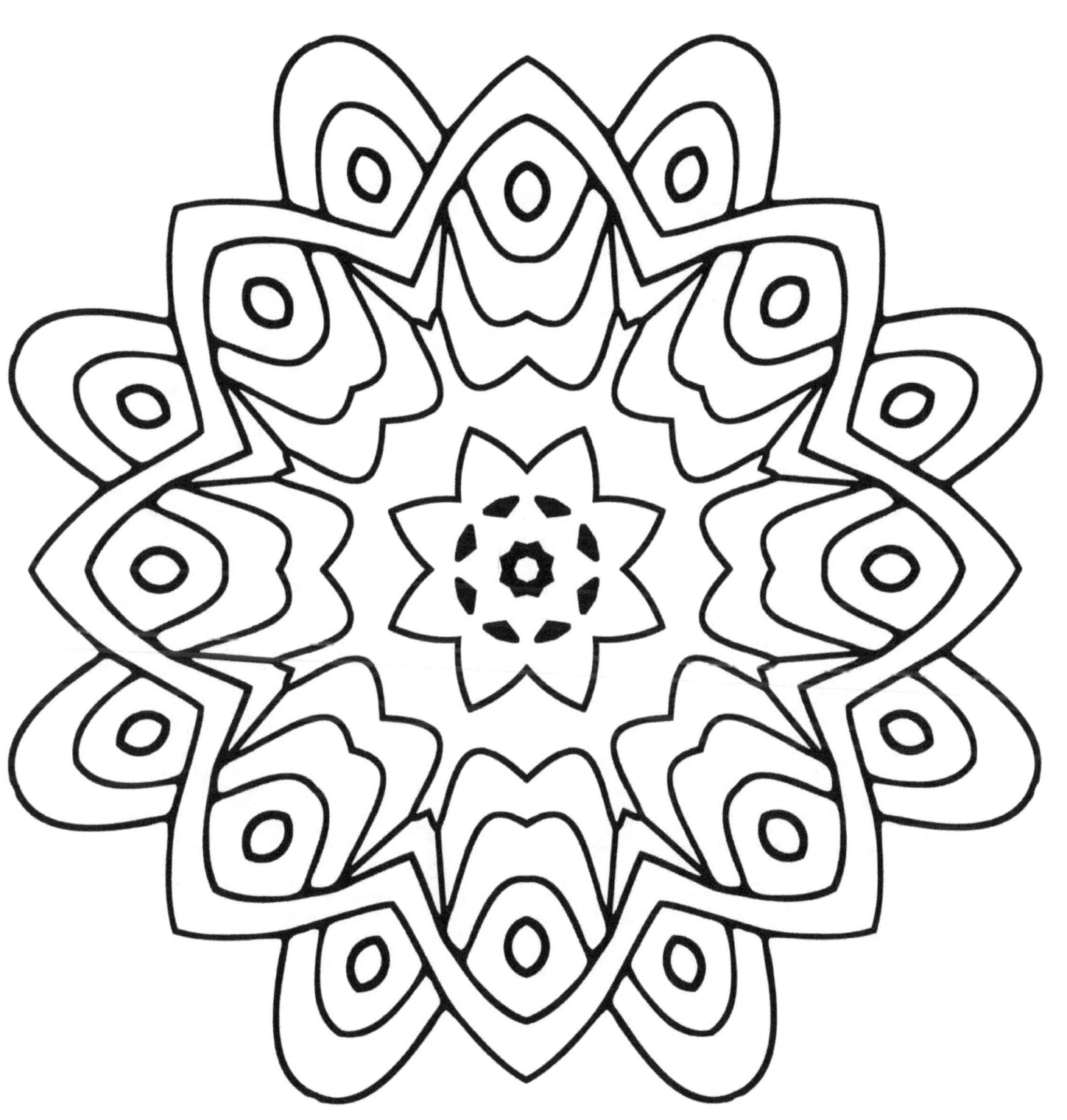

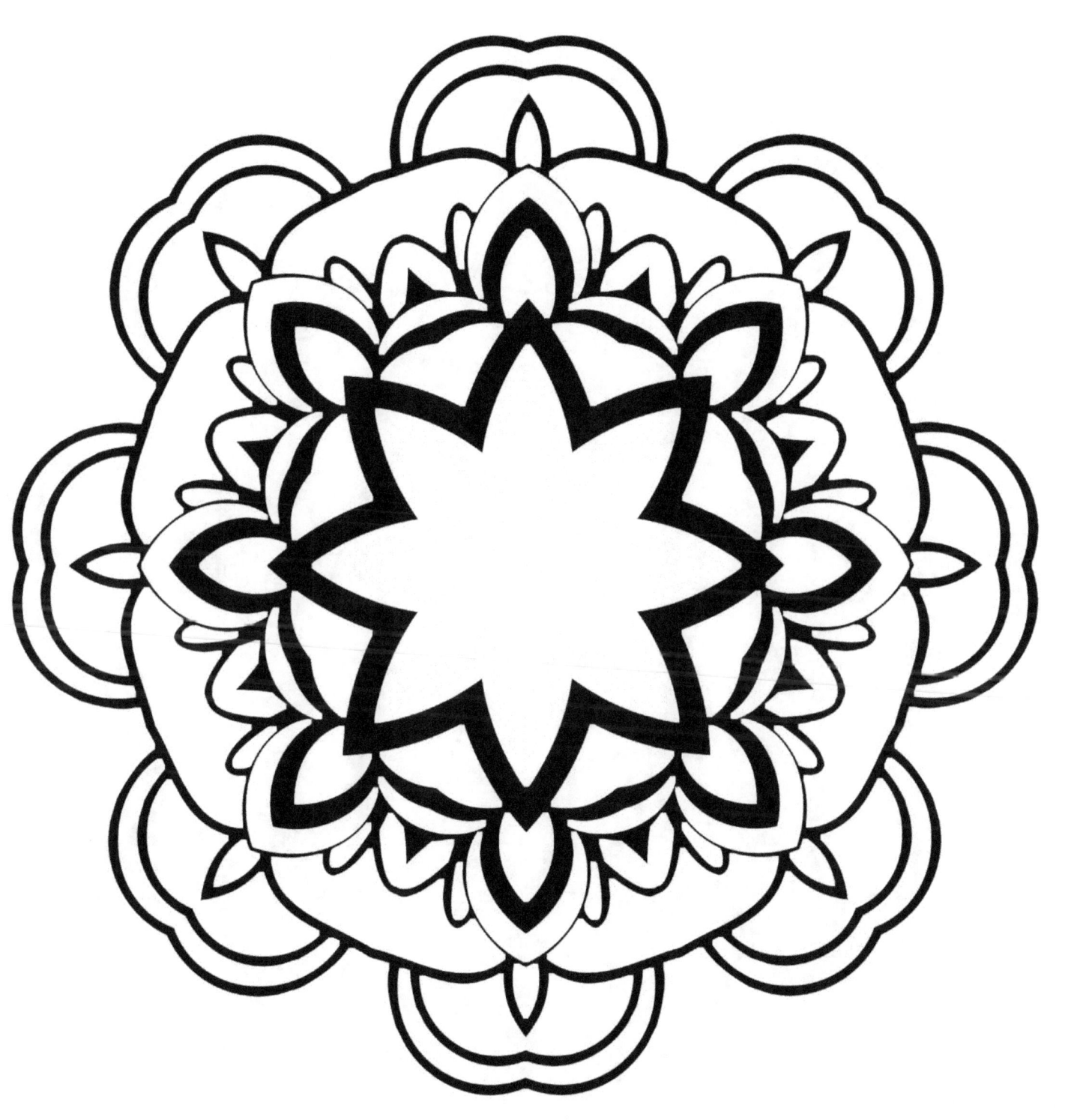

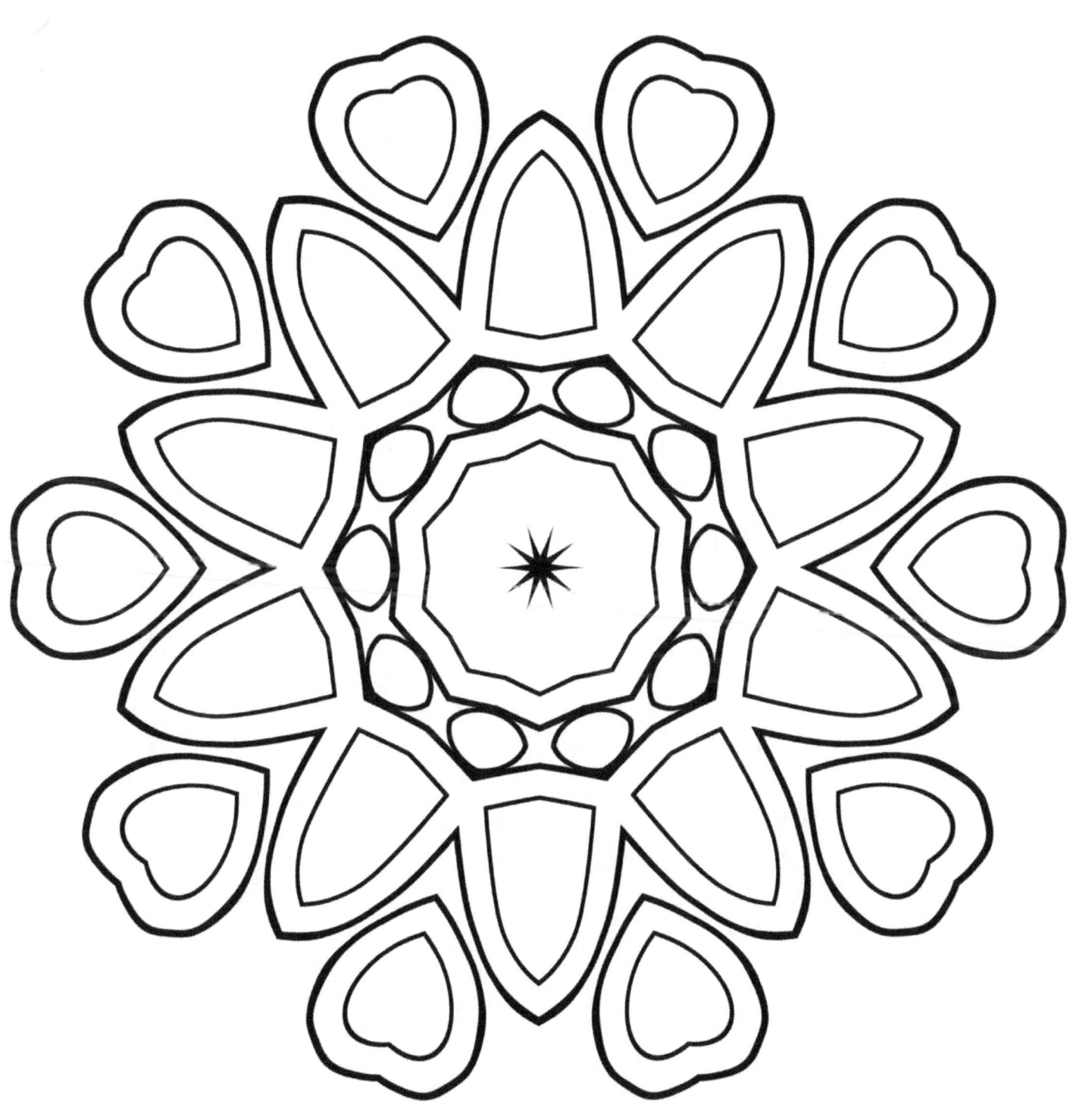

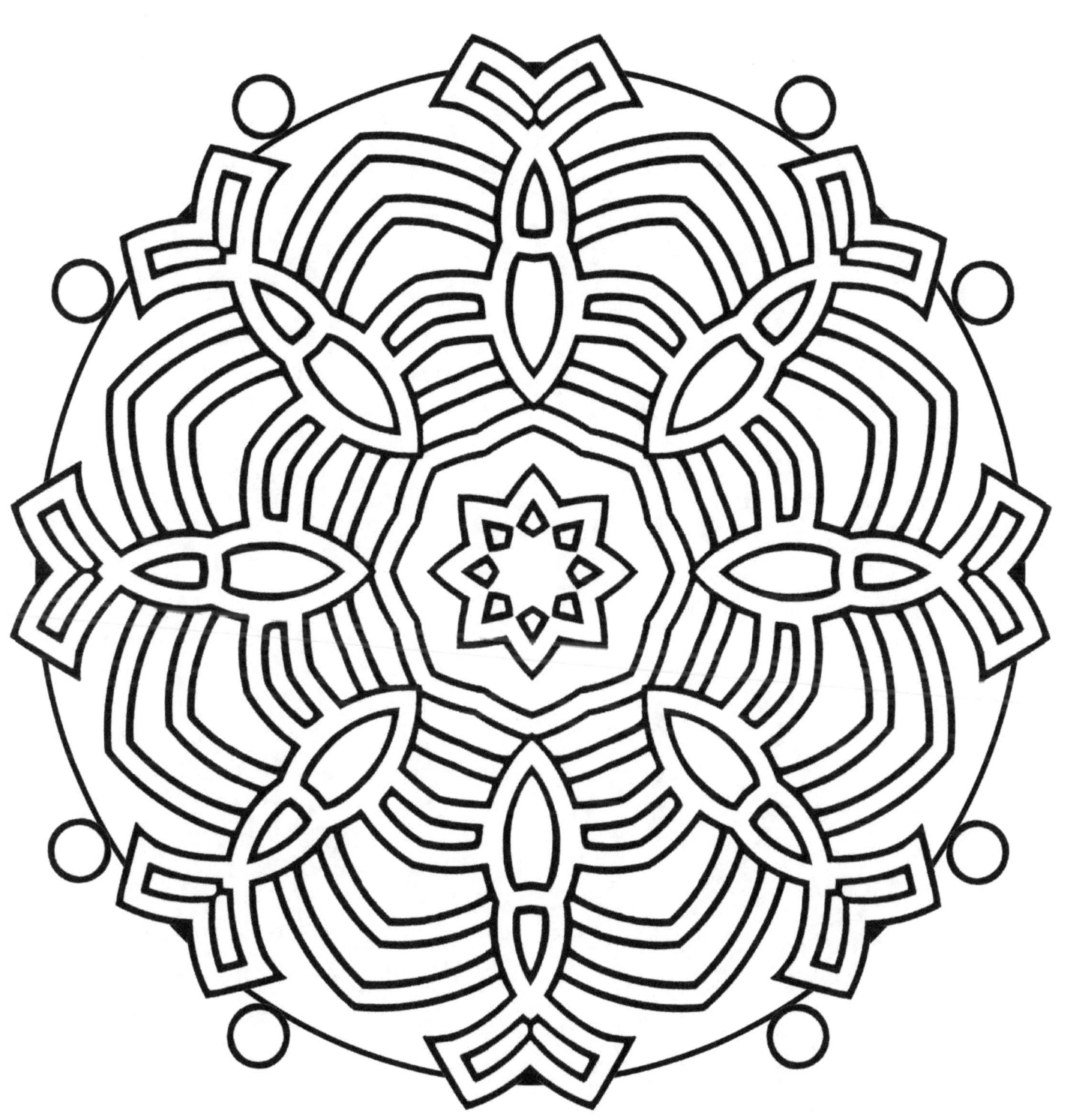

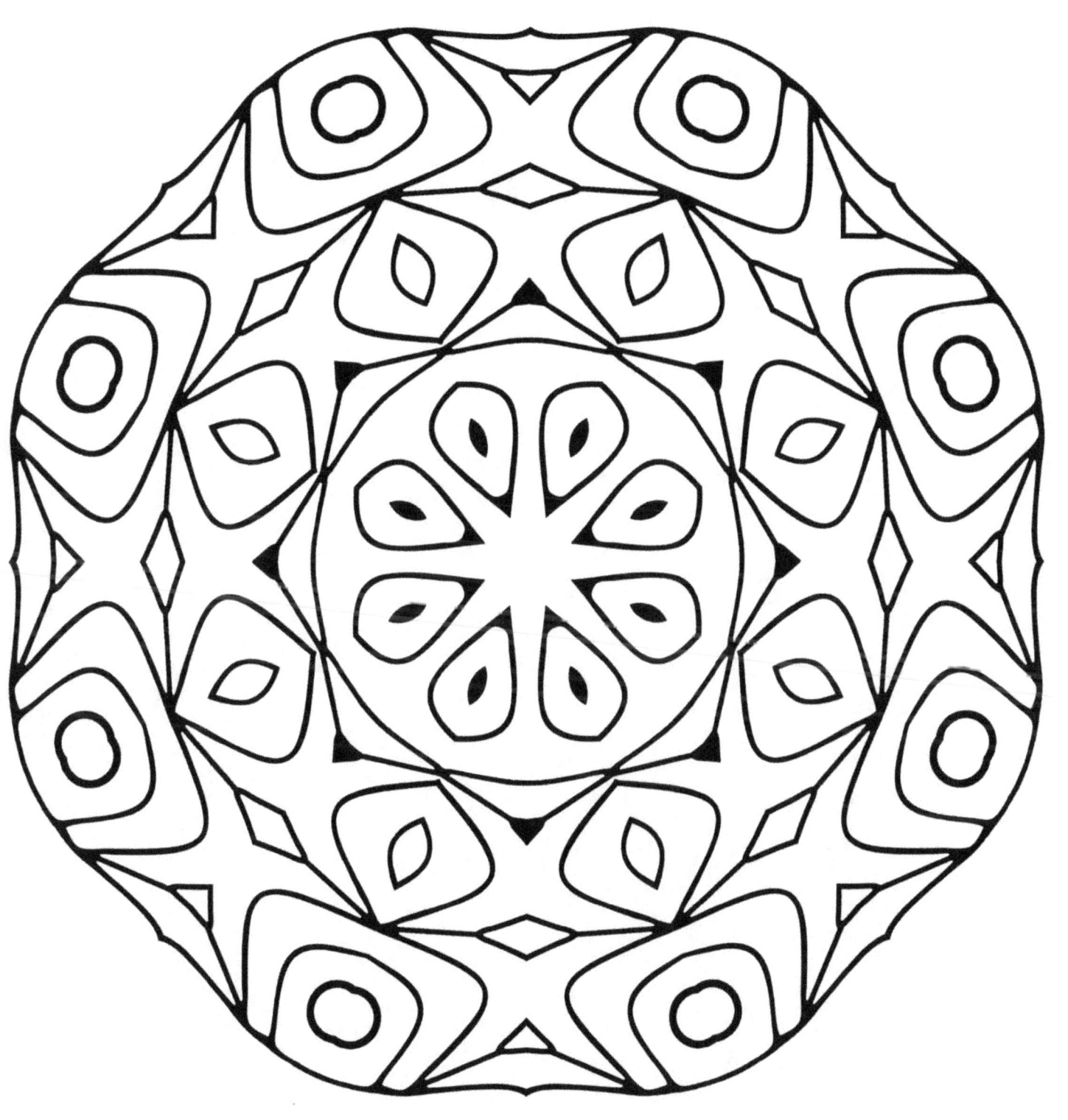

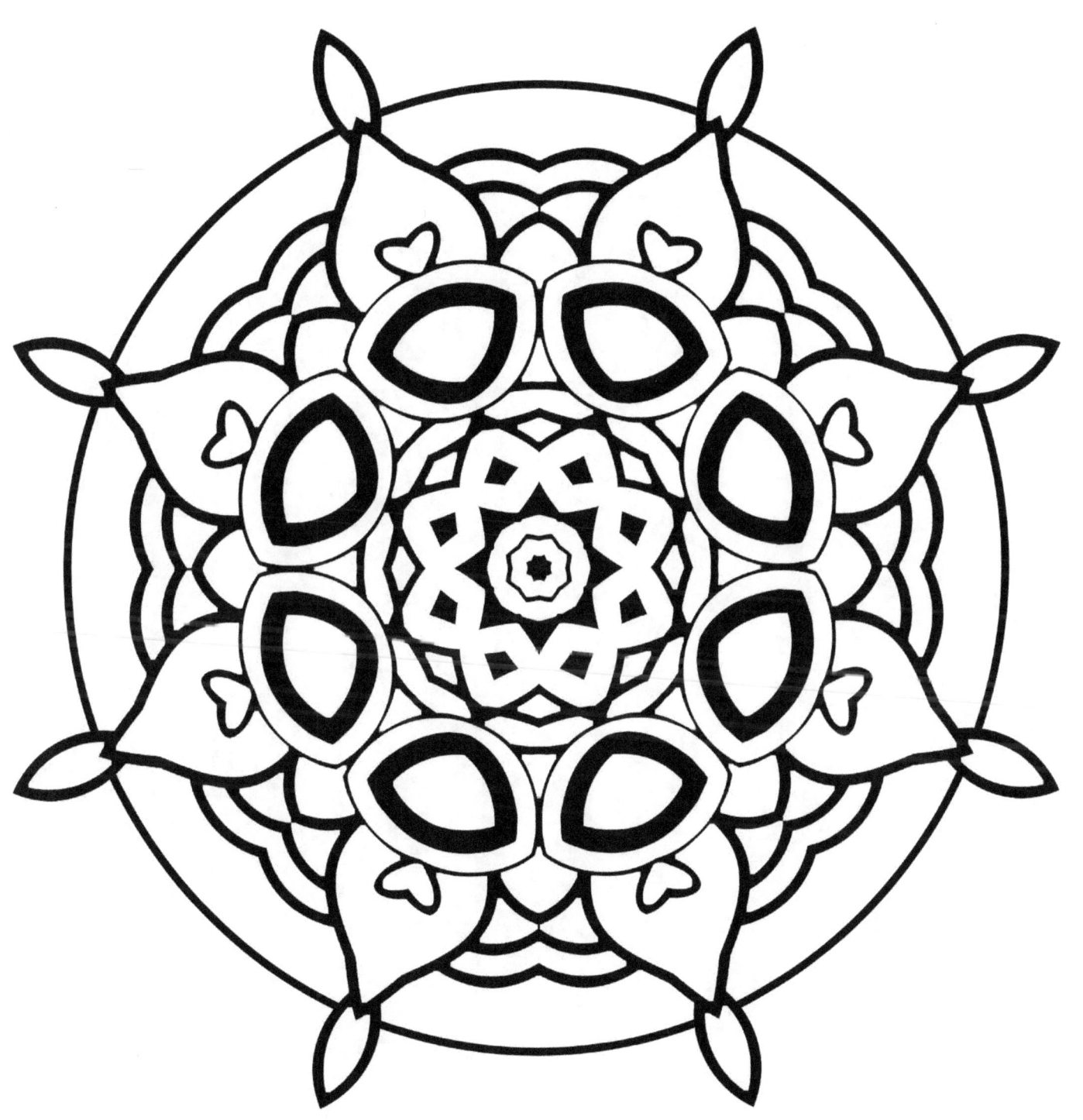

Easy Mandalas
Adults Coloring Book

I have prepared this coloring book for adults keeping in mind beginners, seniors and individuals with low vision. I have included thirty one delightful, one sided illustrations to color as a relaxing and enjoyable pastime. All the mandalas are designed in bolder print and many of them have floral and heart patterns.

Enjoy.

Samantha Moore

About Samantha Moore
Since childhood artist Samantha Moore has been experimenting with colors and their influence on mood and relaxation. She has a degree in Graphic Design, a diploma in Art History and is a Reiki certified therapist.

Copyright © 2016 L. Romo. All rights reserved. With the exception of photocopying for personal use and book review, no part of this book may be reproduced in any form without the written permission of the copyright owner.

Easy Mandalas
Adults Coloring Book

ISBN-13: 978-1539053408
ISBN-10: 1539053407

www.ingramcontent.com/pod-product-compliance
Lightning Source LLC
Chambersburg PA
CBHW080540190526
45169CB00007B/2571